Freshwater Fish of the

Carolinas

FIELD GUIDE

T0126253

by Dave Bosanko

Adventure Publications, Inc.
Cambridge, MN

Edited by Brett Ortler

Illustration credits by artist and page number:

Cover illustrations: Stiped Bass (main) and Bluegill (upper front cover and back cover) by Duane Raver/USFWS

Timothy Knepp/USFWS: 92 (main), 94 **Julie Martinez:** 40, 56, 60 (bottom), 78, 80, 112, 170 **MyFWC.com/fishing:** 11 **Duane Raver/USFWS:** 10, 18, 24, 26, 28, 30, 32, 34, 36, 42, 44, 46, 48, 62, 66, 86, 98, 100, 102 (main), 104, 116 (both), 118, 130, 134, 138, 140, 142, 144, 148, 150, 152, 154, 160, 162, 164, 166, 168 **Joseph Tomelleri:** 38 (both), 52, 54, 58 (both), 60 (top), 64 (both), 68, 70, 72, 74, 76, 82, 84, 88, 90, 92 (inset), 96, 102 (inset), 106 (all), 108, 110, 114, 120, 122, 124, 126, 128, 132, 136, 146, 156, 158

10 9 8 7 6 5 4 3 2

Freshwater Fish of the Carolinas Field Guide
Copyright © 2009 by Dave Bosanko
Published by Adventure Publications
An imprint of AdventureKEEN
310 Garfield Street South
Cambridge, Minnesota 55008
(800) 678-7006
www.adventurepublications.net
Printed in China
ISBN 978-1-59193-217-8 (pbk.)

TABLE OF CONTENTS

Bowfin Family————————————————

Catfish Family————————————————

Cavefish Family————————————————

HOW TO USE THIS BOOK

Your *Fish of the Carolinas Field Guide* is designed to make it easy to identify more than 70 species of the most common and important fish in North and South Carolina and learn fascinating facts about each species' range, natural history and more.

The fish are organized by family, such as Catfish (*Ictaluridae*), Perch (*Percidae*), and Sunfish (*Centrarchidae*), which are listed in alphabetical order. Within these families, individual species are arranged alphabetically in their appropriate groups. For example, members of the Sunfish family are divided into Black Bass, Crappie and True Sunfish groups. For a detailed list of fish families and individual species, turn to the Table of Contents (page 3); the Index (page 176) provides a reference guide to fish by common name (such as Lake Trout) and other common terms for the species.

Fish Identification

Determining a fish's body shape is the first step to identifying it. Each fish family usually exhibits one or sometimes two basic outlines. Catfish have long, stout bodies with flattened heads, barbels or "whiskers" around the mouth, a relatively tall but narrow dorsal fin and an adipose fin. There are two forms of Sunfish: the flat, round, plate-like outline we see in Bluegills and the torpedo or "fusiform" shape of Largemouth Bass.

In this field guide you can quickly identify a fish by first matching its general body shape to one of the fish family silhouettes listed in the Table of Contents (pp. 3-7). From there, turn to that family's section and use the illustrations and text descriptions to identify your fish. Example Pages (pp. 22-23) are provided to explain how the information is presented in each two-page spread.

For some species, the illustration will be enough to identify your catch, but it is important to note that your fish may not look exactly like the artwork. Fish frequently change colors. Males that are brightly colored during the spawning season may show muted coloration at other times. Likewise, bass caught in muddy streams show much less pattern than those taken from clear lakes—and all fish lose some of their markings and color when removed from the water.

Most fish are similar in appearance to one or more other species—often, but not always, within the same family. For example, the Redeye Bass is remarkably similar to the Spotted Bass. To accurately identify such look-alikes, check the inset illustrations and accompanying notes below the main illustration, under the "Similar Species" heading.

Throughout *Fish of the Carolinas* we use basic biological and fisheries management terms that refer to physical characteristics or conditions of fish and their environment, such as dorsal fin or turbid water. For your convenience, these are listed and defined in the Glossary (pp. 172-175), along with other handy fish-related terms and their definitions.

Understanding such terminology will help you make sense of reports on state and federal research, fish population surveys, lake assessments, management plans and other important fisheries documents.

FISH ANATOMY

It's much easier to identify fish if you know the names of the different parts of a fish. For example, it's easier to use the term "adipose fin" to indicate the small, soft, fleshy flap on a Catfish's back than to try to describe it. The following illustrations point out the basic parts of a fish; the accompanying text defines these characteristics.

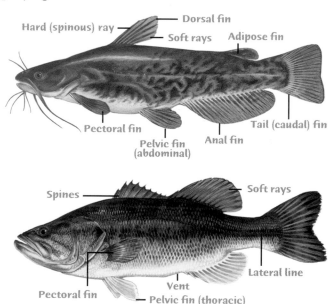

Fins are made up of bony structures that support a membrane. There are three kinds of bony structures in fins: **Soft rays** are flexible fin supports and are often branched.

Spines are stiff, often sharp, supports that are not jointed. **Hard rays** are stiff, pointed, barbed structures that can be raised or lowered. Catfish are famous for their hard rays, which are often mistakenly called spines. Sunfish have soft rays associated with spines to form a prominent dorsal fin.

Fins are named by their position on the fish. The **dorsal fin** is on top along the midline. A few species have another fin on their back, called an **adipose fin**. This small, fleshy protuberance located between the dorsal fin and the tail is distinctive of catfish, trout and salmon. **Pectoral fins** are found on each side of the fish near the gills. The **anal fin** is located along the midline, on the fish's bottom or *ventral* side. There is also a paired set of fins on the bottom of the fish, called the **pelvic fins**. These can be in the thoracic position (just below the pectoral fins) or farther back on the stomach, in the **abdominal position**. The tail is known as the **caudal fin**.

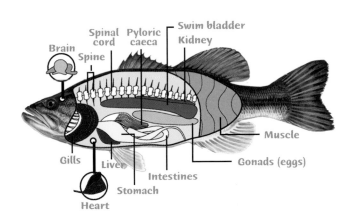

Eyes—In general, fish have good eyesight. They can see color, but vary in terms of how much light they require to see well. For example, Walleyes see well in low light, whereas Bluegills have excellent daytime vision but see poorly at night, making them vulnerable to predation.

Nostrils—A pair of nostrils, or nares, is used to detect odors in the water. Eels and catfishes have particularly well-developed senses of smell.

Mouth—The shape of the mouth is a clue to what the fish eats. The larger the food it consumes, the larger the mouth.

Teeth—Not all fish have teeth, but those that do have mouth gear designed to help them feed. Gars, Pickerels and Bowfins have sharp canine teeth for grabbing and holding prey. Minnows have *pharyngeal* teeth—located in the throat—for grinding.

Catfish have *cardiform* teeth, which feel like a rough patch in the front of the mouth. Bass have patches of *vomerine* teeth on the roof of their mouth.

Swim Bladder—Almost all fish have a swim bladder, a balloon-like organ that helps the fish regulate its buoyancy.

Lateral Line—This sensory organ helps the fish detect movement in the water (to help avoid predators or capture prey) as well as water currents and pressure changes. It consists of fluid-filled sacs with hair-like sensors, which are open to the water through a row of pores in their skin along each side—creating a visible line along the fish's side.

FISH NAMES

A Shellcracker is a Shellcracker in both North and South Carolina, but in the northern parts of its range, Indianans call it a Redear Sunfish. In other regions it's known as stumpknocker or yellow bream. Because common names may vary regionally, and even change for different sizes of the same species, scientific names are used that are exactly the same around the world. Each species has only one correct scientific name that can be recognized anywhere, in any language. The Largemouth Bass is *Micropterus salmoides* from Charleston to Tokyo. Scientific names are made up of Greek or Latin words that often describe the species. There are two parts to a scientific name: the generic or "genus," which is capitalized (*Micropterus*), and the specific name, which is not capitalized (*salmoides*). Both are always written in italic text or underlined. A species' genus represents a group of closely related fish. The Largemouth and Smallmouth Bass are in the same genus, so they share the generic name *Micropterus*. But each fish has a different specific name, *salmoides* for Largemouth Bass, *dolomieu* for the Smallmouth Bass.

ABOUT FISH OF THE CAROLINAS

The Carolinas are very diverse geologically, with mountains in the west, coastal lowlands along the Atlantic, and sloping piedmont in between. These complex landforms foster an abundance of fresh water; there are clear mountain brooks, slow meandering streams and large rivers, as well as mountain lakes, large impoundments and small farm ponds. Along the coast, there are innumerable backwaters that are freshwater or slightly brackish. All of this water provides unlimited habitat for fish.

There are over 200 species of fish in the Carolinas that live in fresh water or enter fresh water to spawn. Of these, over 80 species are represented in this book. About 30 of these fish are commonly targeted by fishermen and another 40 or so are of interest to anyone who spends time near the water. Some of these fish are baitfish and others are included as they have interesting characteristics that are fun to learn about.

FREQUENTLY ASKED QUESTIONS

What is a fish?

Fish are aquatic, typically cold-blooded animals that have backbones, gills and fins.

Are all fish cold-blooded?

All freshwater fish are cold-blooded. Recently, it has been discovered that some members of the saltwater Tuna family are warm-blooded. Whales and Bottlenose Dolphins are also warm-blooded, but they are mammals, not fish.

Do all fish have scales?

No. Most fish have scales that look like those on the Common Goldfish. A few, such as Alligator Gar, have scales that resemble armor plates. Catfish have no scales at all.

How do fish breathe?

A fish takes in water through its mouth and forces it through its gills, where a system of fine membranes absorbs oxygen from the water and releases carbon dioxide. Gills cannot pump air efficiently over these membranes, which quickly dry out and stick together. Fish should never be out of the water longer than you can hold your breath.

Can fish breathe air?

Some species can; gars have a modified swim bladder that acts like a lung. Fish that can't breathe air may die when dissolved oxygen in the water falls below critical levels.

How do fish swim?

Fish swim by contracting bands of muscles on alternate sides of their body so the tail is whipped rapidly from side to side. Pectoral and pelvic fins are used mainly for stability when a fish hovers, but are sometimes used during rapid bursts of forward motion.

Do all fish look like fish?

Most do and are easily recognizable as fish. The eels and lampreys are fish, but they look like snakes. Sculpins look like little goblins with bat wings.

Where can you find fish?

Some fish species can be found in almost any body of water, but not all fish are found everywhere. Each species has adapted to exploit a particular habitat. A species may move around within its home water, sometimes migrating hundreds of miles between lakes, rivers and tributary streams. Some movements, such as spawning migrations, are seasonal and very predictable. Fish may also move horizontally from one area to another, or vertically in the water column, in response to changes in environmental conditions and food availability. In addition, many fish have daily travel patterns. By studying a species' habitat, food and spawning information in this book—and understanding how it interacts with other fish—it is possible to guess where one can find it in any lake, stream or river.

FISH DISEASES

Fish are susceptible to various parasites, infections and diseases. Some diseases have little effect on fish populations while others may have a devastating impact. While fish diseases can't be transmitted to humans, they may render the fish inedible. To prevent the spread of such diseases, care should be taken in not transferring diseased fish from one body of water to another. Information on freshwater fish diseases in the Carolinas can be found at the respective state's Department of Natural Resources website.

North Carolina: http://www.enr.state.nc.us/

South Carolina: http://www.dnr.sc.gov/

INVASIVE SPECIES

While some introduced species have great recreational value, many exotic species have caused problems. Never move fish, water or vegetation from one lake or stream to another, and always follow state laws. Details about invasive species are available at the North Carolina Department of Environmental and Natural Resources (www.ncwildlife.org) and the South Carolina Department of Natural Resources (www.dnr.sc.gov).

FUN WITH FISH

There are many ways to enjoy the Fish of the Carolinas, from reading about them in this book to watching them in the wild. Hands-on activities are also popular. Many resident and non-resident anglers enjoy pursuing game fish. The sport offers a great chance to enjoy the outdoors with friends and family, and in many cases, bring home a healthy meal of fresh fish.

Proceeds from license sales, along with special taxes anglers pay on fishing supplies and motorboat fuel, fund the majority of fish management efforts, including fish surveys, the development of special regulations and stocking programs. The sport also has a huge impact on the economy of the Carolinas, supporting thousands of jobs in fishing, tourism and related industries.

CATCH-AND-RELEASE FISHING

Selective harvest (keeping some fish to eat and releasing the rest) and total catch-and-release fishing allow anglers to enjoy the sport without harming the resource. Catch-and-release is especially important with certain species and sizes of fish, and waters where biologists are trying to improve the fishery by protecting large predators, adult fish, or fish of breeding age. The fishing regulations and information available at your local fisheries offices are excellent sources of advice on which fish to keep and which to release. Catch-and-release is only truly successful if the fish survives. Follow these helpful tips to reduce the chances of post-release mortality.

• Play and land fish quickly.

- Wet your hands before touching a fish, to avoid removing its protective slime coating.

- Handle the fish gently and keep it in the water if possible.

- Do not hold the fish by the eye sockets or gills. Hold it horizontally and support its belly.

- If a fish is deeply hooked, cut the line so at least an inch hangs outside the mouth. This helps the hook lie flush when the fish takes in food.

- Circle hooks may help reduce deeply hooked fish.

- Don't fish deep in water unless you plan to keep your catch.

FISH MEASUREMENT

Fish are measured in three ways: standard length, fork length and total length. The first two are more accurate, because tails are often damaged or worn down. Total length is used in slot limits.

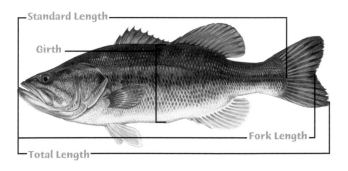

The following formulas estimate the weight of popular game fish. Lengths are in inches; weight is in pounds.

Formulas

Bass weight = (length x length x girth) / 1,200
Pike weight = (length x length x length) / 3,500
Sunfish weight = (length x length x length) / 1,200
Trout weight = (length x girth x girth) / 800
Walleye weight = (length x length x length) / 2,700

For example, let's say that you catch a 16-inch Walleye. Using the formula for Walleyes above: (16 x 16 x 16) divided by 2,700 = 1.5 pounds. Your Walleye would weigh approximately 1.5 pounds.

FISH CONSUMPTION ADVISORIES

Most fish are safe to eat, but pollutants are a valid concern. North and South Carolina routinely monitor contaminant levels and issue advisories and recommendations about eating sport fish caught in the wild.

North Carolina Department of Health: www.epi.state.nc.us.

South Carolina Department of Health: www.scdhec.net.

NORTH CAROLINA STATE RECORD FISH

SPECIES	WEIGHT (LBS.-OZ.)	WHERE CAUGHT	YEAR
Bass, Largemouth	15-4	Farm pond, Union Co.	1991
Bass, Roanoke	2-11	Fishing Creek, Nash Co.	1994
Bass, Rock	1-14	Deep River	1998
Bass, Smallmouth	10-2	Hiwassee Reservoir	1951
Bass, Spotted	6-5	Lake Norman	2003
Bass, Striped	54-2	Hiwassee Reservoir	1991
Bass, Striped Hybrid	17-7	Lake Chatuge	1996
Bass, White	5-14	Kerr Reservoir	1986
Bluegill	4-5	Henderson County	1967
Bowfin	17-15	Black River	1997
Buffalo, Smallmouth	88-0	Lake Wylie	1993
Bullhead, Brown	3-12	Black Hall Creek, Duplin Co.	1997
Bullhead, Yellow	2-12	Little Withlacoochee River	1955
Carp, Common	48-0	Private Pond, Mecklenburg Co.	1986
Carp, Grass	68-12	Summerlins Pond	1998
Catfish, Blue	89-0	Badin Lake	2006
Catfish, Channel	18-8	Neuse River	2007
Catfish, Flathead	78-0	Cape Fear River	2005
Catfish, White	13-0	Lake James	1990
Crappie, Black	4-15	Asheboro City Lake #4	1980
Crappie, White	1-13	Lake Norman	2007
Drum, Freshwater	22-0	Kerr Lake	2006
Flier	1-5	Private Pond	1990
Gar, Longnose	19-10.5	Rock Quarry Lakes	2006
Muskellunge	41-8	Lake Adger	2001
Muskellunge, Tiger	33-8	Lake James	1988
Perch, White	2-15	Falls of Neuse Reservoir	2001
Perch, Yellow	2-9	Indian Creek	1990
Pickerel, Chain	8-0	Gaston Reservoir	1968
Pickerel, Redfin	2-4	Gallberry Swamp	1997
Pike, Northern	11-13	Lake James	1978
Salmon, Kokanee	3-1	Nantahala River	2007
Sauger	5-15	Norman Lake	1971
Shad, American	7-15	Tar River	1974
Shad, Hickory	4-1	Pitchkettle Creek	2004
Sunfish, Green	1-2	Pond at Butner Falls	2006
Sunfish, Pumpkinseed	1-6	Trent River	2003
Sunfish, Redbreast	1-12	Big Swamp, Baldwin Co.	1983
Sunfish, Redear	4-6	Lookout Shoals Lake	1988

SPECIES	WEIGHT (LBS.-OZ.)	WHERE CAUGHT	YEAR
Trout, Brook	7-7	Black River	1980
Trout, Brown	24-10	Raven Fork River	1980
Trout, Rainbow	20-3	Horsepasture River	2006
Walleye	13-8	Lake Chatuge	1986
Warmouth	1-13	McLeods Pond, Richmond Co.	1976

SOUTH CAROLINA STATE RECORD FISH

SPECIES	WEIGHT (LBS.-OZ.)	WHERE CAUGHT	YEAR
Bass, Largemouth	16-2	Lake Marion	1949
Bass, Redeye	5-2.5	Lake Jocassee	2001
Bass, Smallmouth	9-7	Lake Jocassee	2001
Bass, Spotted	8-2	Lake Jocassee	1996
Bass, Striped	59-8	Lake Hartwell	2002
Bass, Striped Hybrid	20-6	Savannah River	1978
Bass, White	5-4.8	Lake Murray	2006
Bluegill	3-4	Lancaster Co.	1973
Bowfin	21-8	Forest Lake	1980
Bullhead	6-3	Edisto River	1973
Catfish, Blue	109-4	Tailrace Channel	1991
Catfish, Channel	58-0	Lake-Moultrie	1964
Catfish, Flathead	79-4	Santee Cooper Diversion Channel	2001
Catfish, White	9-15	Lake Murray	1986
Crappie, Black	5-0	Lake Moultrie	1957
Crappie, White	5-1	Lake Murray	1949
Flier	1-4	Hemingway	1977
Muskellunge	22-8	Broad River	2004
Perch, Yellow	3-4	Lake Keowee	1979
Perch, White	1-13.5	Lake Murray	1986
Pickerel, Chain	6-4	Chessey Creek	1981
Pickerel, Redfin	1-8.8	Bluff Lake	1983
Sauger	4-7	Lake Thurmond	1985
Shad, American	7-0	Santee River	1985
Sunfish, Pumpkinseed	2-4	North Saluda River	1997
Sunfish, Redbreast	2-0	Lumber River	1975
Sunfish, Redear	5-7	Diversion Canal	1998
Trout, Brook	2-6	Chattooga River	1979
Trout, Brown	17-9.5	Lake Jocassee	1987
Trout, Rainbow	11-5	Lake Jocassee	1993
Walleye	10-0	Lake Russell	1993
Warmouth	5-0	Lake Moultrie	1957

These pages explain how the information is presented for each fish.

SAMPLE FISH ILLUSTRATION

Description: brief summary of physical characteristics to help you identify the fish, such as coloration and markings, body shape, fin size and placement

Similar Species: list of other fish that look similar and the pages on which they can be found; includes detailed inset drawings (below) highlighting key physical traits such as markings, mouth size or shape and fin characteristics to help you distinguish this fish from similar species

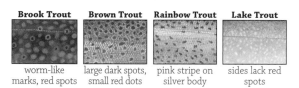

Brook Trout	**Brown Trout**	**Rainbow Trout**	**Lake Trout**
worm-like marks, red spots	large dark spots, small red dots	pink stripe on silver body	sides lack red spots

SAMPLE COMPARISON ILLUSTRATIONS

22

COMMON NAME
Scientific Name

Other Names: common terms or nicknames you may hear to describe this species

Habitat: environment where the fish is found (such as streams, rivers, small or large lakes, fast-flowing or still water, in or around vegetation, near shore, in clear water)

Range: geographic distribution, starting with the fish's overall range, followed by state-specific information

Food: what the fish eats most of the time (such as crustaceans, insects, fish, plankton)

Reproduction: timing of and behavior during the spawning period (such as dates and water temperatures, migration information, preferred spawning habitat, type of nest if applicable, colonial or solitary nester, parental care for eggs or fry)

Average Size: average length or range of length, average weight or range of weight

Records: state—the state record for this species, location and year; North American—the North American record for this species, location and year (from the National Fresh Water Fishing Hall of Fame)

Notes: interesting natural history information; this can include unique behaviors, remarkable features, sporting and table quality, details on annual migrations, seasonal patterns or population trends

Description: brownish-green back and sides with a white belly; long, stout body; rounded tail; continuous dorsal fin; bony plates covering head; males have a large "eye" spot at the base of the tail

Similar Species: American Eel (pg. 44), Sea Lamprey (pg. 58)

Bowfin	American Eel	Bowfin	Sea Lamprey
one dorsal fin, short anal fin	fused dorsal, tail and anal fin	no barbel on chin	mouth is a sucking disk

BOWFIN

Amia calva

Amiidae

Other Names: dogfish, grindle, mudfish, cypress trout, lake lawyer, beaverfish

Habitat: deep waters associated with weedbeds in warmwater lakes and rivers; feeds in shallow weeds

Range: the Mississippi River drainage east and south from Texas to Florida; common throughout the coastal plain of the Carolinas and introduced into a few Piedmont and mountain reservoirs in North Carolina

Food: fish, crayfish

Reproduction: when water exceeds 61 degrees, male removes vegetation to build a nest in sand or gravel; one or more females deposit up to 5,000 eggs; male tenaciously guards the nest and "ball" of young

Average Size: 12 to 24 inches, 2 to 5 pounds

Records: NC—17 pounds, 15 ounces, Black River, 1997; SC—21 pounds, 8 ounces, Forest Lake, 1980; North American—21 pounds, 8 ounces, Forest Lake, South Carolina, 1980

Notes: A voracious predator, the Bowfin prowls shallow weedbeds preying on anything that moves. Once thought detrimental to game fish populations, it is now considered an asset in controlling rough fish and stunted game fish. An air breather that tolerates low oxygen levels, the Bowfin can survive buried in mud for short periods during droughts. While most anglers consider the Bowfin a nuisance, some anglers seek it out for its fighting ability.

Description: yellowish-brown upper body; mottled back and sides; barbels around mouth; adipose fin; scaleless skin; rounded tail; well-defined barbs on the pectoral spines

Similar Species: Yellow Bullhead (pg. 28), White Catfish (pg. 36), Madtoms (pg. 38)

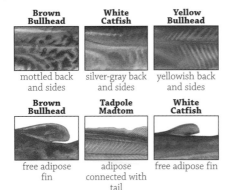

Brown Bullhead	White Catfish	Yellow Bullhead
mottled back and sides	silver-gray back and sides	yellowish back and sides

Brown Bullhead	Tadpole Madtom	White Catfish
free adipose fin	adipose connected with tail	free adipose fin

Ictaluridae

BROWN BULLHEAD
Ameiurus nebulosus

Other Names: marbled or speckled bullhead, red cat

Habitat: warm, weedy lakes and sluggish streams

Range: southern Canada through the Great Lakes down the eastern states to Florida, introduced in the West; common throughout the Carolinas

Food: a scavenging opportunist, feeds mostly on insects, fish, fish eggs, snails, and some plant matter

Reproduction: in early summer, males build a nest in shallow water amid vegetation with a sandy or rocky bottom; both sexes guard the eggs and young

Average Size: 8 to 10 inches, 4 ounces to 2 pounds

Records: NC—3 pounds, 12 ounces, Buck Hall Creek, Duplin County, 1997; SC—6 pounds, 3 ounces, Edisto River, 1973; North American—6 pounds, 2 ounces, Pearl River, Mississippi, 1991

Notes: The Brown Bullhead is the most abundant catfish species in the Carolinas and can be found in turbid backwaters as well as in clear lakes and streams. Adults are very involved in rearing their young; first they agitate the eggs, then they guard the black fry, which swim in a tight ball. Like other catfish, Brown Bullheads are nocturnal feeders. They are not strong fighters, but are easy to catch when fishing the bottom with worms as bait. The reddish meat is tasty and fine table fare when taken from clear water.

Description: olive head and back; yellowish-green head and sides; white belly; barbels on lower jaw are pale green or white; adipose fin; scaleless skin; rounded tail

Similar Species: Brown Bullhead (pg. 26), White Catfish (pg. 36)

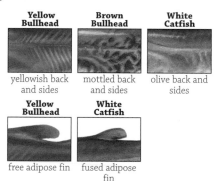

Yellow Bullhead	Brown Bullhead	White Catfish
yellowish back and sides	mottled back and sides	olive back and sides

Yellow Bullhead	White Catfish
free adipose fin	fused adipose fin

YELLOW BULLHEAD

Ameiurus natalis

Ictaluridae

Other Names: white-whiskered bullhead, yellow cat

Habitat: warm, weedy lakes and sluggish streams

Range: the southern Great Lakes through the eastern half of the U.S. to the Gulf and into Mexico, introduced in the West; common throughout the Carolinas

Food: scavenging opportunist, feeds on insects, crayfish, snails, small fish, some plant matter

Reproduction: from late spring to early summer, male builds a nest in shallow water amid vegetation and a soft bottom; both sexes guard the eggs and young

Average Size: 8 to 10 inches, 1 to 2 pounds

Records: NC—none; SC—unspecified bullhead, 6 pounds, 3 ounces, Edisto River, 1973; North American—4 pounds, 15 ounces, Ogeechee River, Georgia, 2003

Notes: The Yellow Bullhead is the bullhead species least tolerant of turbidity and is more commonly found in clear streams or ponds. Bullheads feed by "taste," locating food by following chemical trails through the water. This ability can be greatly diminished in polluted water, impairing the bullhead's ability to find food. The Yellow Bullhead is less likely than other bullhead species to overpopulate a lake and become stunted. Yellow Bullheads are easily caught with worms or cut bait throughout the day, but they are more active at night. The creamy, white flesh is firm and tasty when the fish are taken from clean water.

29

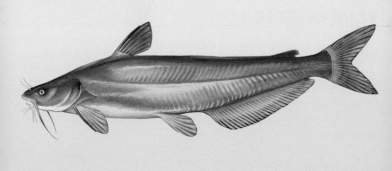

Description: body pale blue to slate gray; hump in back at dorsal fin; long anal fin with straight rear edge; forked tail; adipose fin; no scales; chin barbels

Similar Species: Channel Catfish (pg. 32), White Catfish (pg. 36)

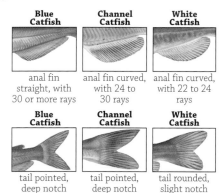

Blue Catfish	Channel Catfish	White Catfish
anal fin straight, with 30 or more rays	anal fin curved, with 24 to 30 rays	anal fin curved, with 22 to 24 rays

Blue Catfish	Channel Catfish	White Catfish
tail pointed, deep notch	tail pointed, deep notch	tail rounded, slight notch

BLUE CATFISH

Ictalurus furcatus

Other Names: humpback, river, forktail, great blue, silver, chucklehead or Missouri cat, blue fulton

Habitat: deep pools of large rivers with hard bottoms and moderate to strong current, a few reservoirs

Range: the Mississippi River watershed and into Mexico; in NC, Cape Fear, the South and Black River systems; in SC, the Catawba River

Food: fish, crayfish

Reproduction: spawns when water reaches the low 80s; male builds and defends a nest in undercut banks or other sheltered areas; males guard young for a short period

Average Size: 20 to 30 inches, 15 to 25 pounds

Records: NC—89 pounds, Badin Lake, 2006; SC—109 pounds, 4 ounces, Tailrace Channel, 1991; North American—124 pounds, Mississippi River, Illinois, 2005

Notes: Blue Catfish are the largest North American catfish and are not native to the Carolinas. Primarily river fish, they prefer fast currents and often congregate in the fast water below power-generating dams and feed on injured fish that pass through the turbines. In a few situations, Blue Catfish populations have been established in large lakes and reservoirs. Smaller Blue Catfish are often mistaken for Channel Catfish or White Catfish, which can have similar coloration. This has led to a great deal of confusion in some fishing contests. Like other catfish species, Blue Catfish have firm, white flesh that is fine table fare.

31

Description: steel gray to silver on the back and sides; white belly; black spots on the sides; large fish lack spots and appear dark olive or slate gray; forked tail; adipose fin; long barbels around mouth

Similar Species: Bullheads (pp. 26-29), White Catfish (pg. 36)

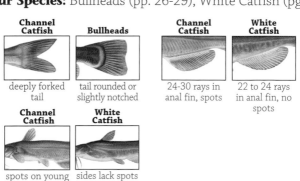

Channel Catfish	**Bullheads**	**Channel Catfish**	**White Catfish**
deeply forked tail	tail rounded or slightly notched	24-30 rays in anal fin, spots	22 to 24 rays in anal fin, no spots

Channel Catfish	**White Catfish**
spots on young fish	sides lack spots

CHANNEL CATFISH
Ictalurus punctatus

Other Names: spotted, speckled or silver catfish, fiddler

Habitat: medium to large streams with deep pools, low to moderate current and sand, gravel or rubble bottom; also found in warm lakes; tolerates turbid (cloudy) conditions

Range: southern Canada through the Midwest into Mexico and Florida, widely introduced; common throughout the Carolinas

Food: insects, crustaceans, fish, some plant matter

Reproduction: matures at 2 to 4 years; in summer when water temperature reaches about 70 to 85 degrees, male builds a nest in a dark, sheltered area; female deposits 2,000 to 21,000 eggs, which hatch in 6 to 10 days; male guards eggs and young until the nest is deserted

Average Size: 12 to 20 inches, 3 to 4 pounds

Records: NC—18 pounds, 8 ounces, Neuse River, 2007; SC—58 pounds, Lake Moultrie, 1964; North American—58 pounds, Santee Cooper Reservoir, South Carolina, 1964

Notes: Channel Catfish are one of the most sought after fish in the South. Like other catfish, Channel Catfish feed both day and night, but serious anglers often pursue them at night. When caught, they put up a strong fight and are fine table fare. Channel Catfish were the first widely farmed fish in the U.S. and are now also raised in Asia for export around the world. Channel Catfish are the only native freshwater American fish commonly found in grocery stores and restaurants throughout the country. **33**

Description: color variable, body and head usually mottled yellow or brown; belly cream to yellow; head broad and flattened; pronounced underbite; adipose fin; chin barbels

Similar Species: Blue Catfish (pg. 30), Channel Catfish (pg. 32)

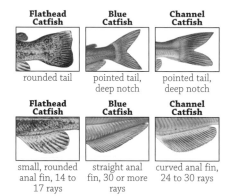

Flathead Catfish	Blue Catfish	Channel Catfish
rounded tail	pointed tail, deep notch	pointed tail, deep notch

Flathead Catfish	Blue Catfish	Channel Catfish
small, rounded anal fin, 14 to 17 rays	straight anal fin, 30 or more rays	curved anal fin, 24 to 30 rays

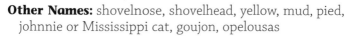

FLATHEAD CATFISH

Pylodictis olivaris

Ictaluridae

Other Names: shovelnose, shovelhead, yellow, mud, pied, johnnie or Mississippi cat, goujon, opelousas

Habitat: deep pools of large rivers and impoundments

Range: the Mississippi River watershed and into Mexico; native only to westward flowing rivers in NC, common in most of the larger rivers of both states

Food: fish, crayfish

Reproduction: spawns when water is 72 to 80 degrees; male builds and defends nest in hollow logs or undercut banks; large females may lay up to 30,000 eggs

Average Size: 20 to 30 inches, 10 to 20 pounds

Records: State—NC—78 pounds, Cape Fear River, 2005; SC—79 pounds, 4 ounces, Santee Cooper Diversion Canal, 2001; North American—123 pounds, Elk River Reservoir, Kansas, 1998

Notes: A large, solitary predator that feeds aggressively on live fish at night. Flatheads are frequently found near log-jams or in deep pools where they like to hide in cavities during the day. Occasionally, Flatheads enter shallow water seeking prey on the surface, but they are more likely to stay in deep water. Flatheads have been introduced in small lakes in an attempt to control stunted panfish populations, with limited success. Some of these introductions result in steep declines in popular game fish populations. A strong, tenacious fighter with firm, white flesh, Flatheads are highly prized by many anglers.

35

Description: bluish-silver body and off-white belly; older fish dark blue with some mottling; forked tail with pointed lobes; lacks scales; adipose fin; white chin barbels

Similar Species: Channel Catfish (pg. 32)

White Catfish	**Channel Catfish**	**White Catfish**	**Channel Catfish**
22 to 24 rays in anal fin, no spots	24 to 30 rays in anal fin	sides lack spots	spots on young fish

WHITE CATFISH

Ameiurus catus

Other Names: silver or weed catfish, whitey

Habitat: fresh to slightly brackish water of coastal streams; shallow lakes with good vegetation and a firm bottom

Range: Maine south to Florida and west to Texas, introduced in some Western states; common throughout the Carolinas

Food: insects, crayfish, small fish, some plant debris

Reproduction: male builds nest in sheltered areas with a sand or gravel bottom when water temperatures reach the high 60s; both sexes guard nest and eggs until fry disperse

Average Size: 10 to 18 inches, 1 to 2 pounds

Records: NC—13 pounds, Lake James, 1990; SC—9 pounds, 15 ounces, Lake Murray, 1986; North American—22 pounds, William Land Park Pond, California, 1994

Notes: The White Catfish is a native species that is stocked in fresh and slightly brackish coastal waters of the Carolinas. In terms of habits, White Catfish share characteristics with Channel Catfish and Bullheads; White Catfish prefer quieter water than Channel Catfish with a somewhat firmer bottom than that sought by Bullheads. They are somewhat less nocturnal than other catfish. In terms of popularity with Carolina fishermen, they are second only to Channel Catfish. They frequent the edge of reed beds and are often caught when still-fishing the bottom near deep water. Large White Catfish put up a good battle and have firm, white flesh with a fine flavor.

MARGINED MADTOM

TADPOLE MADTOM

Description: Margined—gray to tan; protruding upper jaw;
Tadpole—dark olive to brown; dark line on side; jaws even;
fin margins black; both species—large, fleshy head with barbels at mouth; adipose fin connected to tail fin

Similar Species: Bullheads (pp. 26-29), Catfish (pp. 30-37)

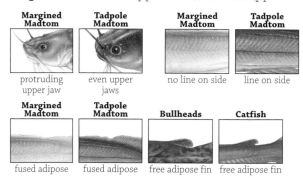

Margined Madtom	Tadpole Madtom	Margined Madtom	Tadpole Madtom
protruding upper jaw	even upper jaws	no line on side	line on side

Margined Madtom	Tadpole Madtom	Bullheads	Catfish
fused adipose	fused adipose	free adipose fin	free adipose fin

MARGINED MADTOM

Noturus insignis

TADPOLE MADTOM *Noturus gyrinus*

Other Names: willow or tadpole cat, tadpole stonecat, river or creek madtom

Habitat: Tadpole—vegetated water near shore in medium to large lakes, Margined—rocky stream creek riffles

Range: Tadpole—the eastern U.S. from the Gulf through the Great Lake states; common in the Carolina coastal plains; Margined—Atlantic slope from New York to Georgia; common in streams throughout the Carolinas except the far west

Food: small invertebrates, algae and other plant matter

Reproduction: both spawn in late spring; females lay eggs under objects such as roots, rocks, logs, or in abandoned crayfish burrows; nest guarded by adults

Average Size: 3 to 4 inches

Records: none

Notes: There are 7 species of small catfish called madtoms that live in the Carolinas. The Margined Madtom, like most species in the family, is a stream fish; the Tadpole Madtom is the exception and prefers lakes and ponds. Madtoms have poison glands under their skin at the base of the dorsal and pectoral fins; these produce a painful burning sensation but will do no lasting damage. Madtoms are hardy little fish and a popular baitfish in some areas. Reportedly, damaging the "slime" coating (by rolling them in sand) to make handling easier reduces their effectiveness as bait.

Description: bicolored, brown above lateral line, creamy white below; 3 dark stripes on sides; flattened head with small eyes; large rounded pectoral fins; no pelvic fins

Similar Species: Eastern Mudminnow (pg. 78)

Swampfish	Eastern Mudminnow
bicolored, no pelvic fins	solid color on sides, pelvic fins

SWAMPFISH

Chologaster cornuta

Other Names: mud or blacktop minnow

Habitat: near or in bottom vegetation of darkly stained water in swamps, creeks and lakes

Range: Atlantic coastal plains from Virginia to east central Georgia; coastal plains of the Carolinas

Food: small crustaceans and aquatic insect larvae

Reproduction: spawns in late spring but little else is known of their breeding behavior

Average Size: 1 to 3 inches

Records: none

Notes: This interesting and attractive member of the cavefish family is adapted to living in the darkly stained waters of swamps and creeks, not caves. Swampfish are secretive, nocturnal bottom dwellers that are never found far from thick vegetation. Adult males develop a small, fleshy appendage on the snout, the function of which is unclear. As with other cavefish species, as the fish matures the anus of the Swampfish migrates forward from the normal position to just under the gills. Swampfish are not often noticed but they can be locally very abundant in roadside ditches and small swamps.

Description: gray back with purple or bronze reflections; silver sides; white underbelly; humped back; dorsal fin extends from hump to near tail; lateral line runs from head through tail

Similar Species: White Bass (pg. 162)

Freshwater Drum	White Bass	Freshwater Drum	White Bass
triangular tail	forked tail	down turned mouth	upturned mouth

FRESHWATER DRUM

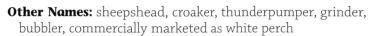

Sciaenidae

Aplodinotus grunniens

Other Names: sheepshead, croaker, thunderpumper, grinder, bubbler, commercially marketed as white perch

Habitat: areas with slow to moderate currents in rivers and streams; shallow lakes with soft bottoms; prefers turbid (cloudy) water

Range: Canada south through the Midwest into eastern Mexico to Guatemala; locally abundant in streams of western North Carolina

Food: small fish, insects, crayfish, clams, mussels

Reproduction: in May and June after water temperatures reach about 66 degrees, schools of drum lay eggs near the surface over sand or gravel; no parental care of fry

Average Size: 10 to 14 inches, 2 to 5 pounds

Records: NC—22 pounds. Kerr Lake, 2006; SC—none; North American—54 pounds, 8 ounces, Nickajack Lake, Tennessee, 1972

Notes: The only freshwater member of a large family of marine fish. Drums are named for a grunting noise that is made by males, primarily to attract females. This noise is occasionally made when a drum is removed from the water and handled. The sound is produced by specialized muscles which are rubbed along the swim bladder. The skull contains two enlarged L-shaped earstones called otoliths that were once prized for jewelry by Native Americans. The flesh is flaky, white and tasty, but easily dries out when cooked due to the low oil content.

43

Description: dark brown on top with yellow sides and white belly; long, snake-like body with large mouth; pectoral fins; gill slits; continuous dorsal, tail and anal fin

Similar Species: Mountain Brook Lamprey (pg. 58), Sea Lamprey (pg. 58)

American Eel	**Sea Lamprey**	**Mountain Brook Lamprey**
continuous dorsal tail, anal fin, no notch in dorsal fin	continuous dorsal tail and anal fin, deeply notched dorsal fin	slightly notched dorsal fin

American Eel	**Sea Lamprey**
pectoral fins	no pectoral fins

AMERICAN EEL

Anguilla rostrata

Anguillidae

Other Names: common, Boston, Atlantic or freshwater eel

Habitat: soft bottoms of medium to large streams, brackish tidewater areas

Range: Atlantic Ocean, eastern and central North America and eastern Central America; any Carolina waters with coastal access

Food: insects, crayfish, small fish

Reproduction: a "catadromous" species that spends most of its life in freshwater, the American Eel returns to the Sargasso Sea in the North Atlantic Ocean to spawn; females lay up to 20 million eggs; adults die after spawning

Average Size: 24 to 36 inches, 1 to 3 pounds

Records: State—none; North American—8 pounds, 8 ounces, Cliff Pond, Massachusetts, 1992

Notes: Leaf-shaped larval eels drift with ocean currents for about a year after hatching in the Sargasso Sea. When they reach river mouths of North and Central America they morph into small eels (elvers). Males remain in the estuaries; females migrate upstream, often hundreds of miles. At maturity (up to 20 years of age) adults return to the Sargasso Sea. The popularity of eels has decreased in the last 100 years, and now there is only a limited commercial harvest and few anglers seek them out. Even so, smoked eels have excellent flavor.

45

Description: olive to brown with dark spots along sides; long, cylindrical profile; single dorsal fin located just above the anal fin; body encased in hard, plate-like scales; snout twice as long as head; needle-sharp teeth on both jaws

Similar Species: none

LONGNOSE GAR

Lepisosteus osseus

Other Names: garfish

Habitat: quiet water of larger rivers and lakes

Range: the central U.S. throughout the Mississippi drainage south into Mexico, a few rivers in the northeast Great Lakes drainage; common in the Carolina coastal plains and less common in rivers in the Tennessee, Pee Dee and Catawba drainages

Food: minnows and other small fish

Reproduction: large, green eggs are deposited in weedy shallows when water temperature reaches the high 60s; using a small disc on the snout, newly hatched gar attach to something solid until their digestive tracts develop enough to allow feeding

Average Size: 14 to 24 inches, 2 to 4 pounds

Records: NC—19 pounds, 10.5 ounces, Rock Quarry Lakes, 2006; SC—none; North American—50 pounds, 5 ounces, Trinity River, Texas, 1954

Notes: Gar belong to a prehistoric family of fish that can breathe air with the aid of a modified swim bladder. This adaptation helps them survive in increasingly polluted, slow-moving rivers and lakes. Gar are a valuable asset in controlling populations of rough fish; they hunt by floating motionless, then make a quick, sideways slash to capture prey. They are tenacious fighters when caught, but their bony jaws make them hard to hook. The flesh is strongly flavored and not popular with most anglers. **47**

Description: blue to blue-green metallic back; silver sides with faint dark stripes; white belly; purple spot just behind the gill, directly above the pectoral fin; large mouth with protruding lower jaw; sharply pointed scales (scutes) along the ventral midline

Similar Species: American Shad (pg. 50), Blueback Herring (pg. 52), Hickory Shad (pg. 56)

Alewife	**American Shad**	**Blueback Herring**	**Hickory Shad**
mouth extends to middle of eye; silver-gray body cavity lining; mouth not below snout	mouth extends to back of eye	black body cavity lining	mouth below snout

ALEWIFE

Alosa pseudoharengus

Other Names: ellwife, sawbelly, golden shad, big-eyed or river herring

Habitat: open water of the Great Lakes and a few inland lakes; coastal waters and streams

Range: the Atlantic Ocean from Labrador to the Carolinas, St. Lawrence River drainage and the Great Lakes; coastal streams of SC and a few coastal streams in northern NC

Food: zooplankton, filamentous algae

Reproduction: in the Great Lakes, spawning takes place in open water of bays and along protected shorelines during early summer; coastal alewives make spring runs up rivers when the water warms to 50 degrees; spawns over sandy bottoms in protected bays

Average Size: landlocked, 4 to 8 inches; marine, 12 to 15 inches

Records: none

Notes: The Alewife is restricted to coastal waters in the Carolinas but is commonly introduced in large impoundments in other states. While the Alewife is not a popular sport fish, there is a small, but persistent, commercial harvest. Those that are caught are primarily taken with nets and smoked, salted, or canned. Larger Alewives are very similar in appearance to Hickory Shad. The Alewife has a pale gray body cavity lining, whereas the Hickory Shad's is silver-white.

Description: silver body and blue-gray back; three or more dark spots on the shoulder; body deep and laterally compressed; large mouth extending to back of eye; sawtooth edge of sharply pointed scales along the belly (scutes)

Similar Species: Alewife (pg. 48), Blueback Herring (pg. 52), Hickory Shad (pg. 56)

American Shad	**Alewife**	**Blueback Herring**	**Hickory Shad**
mouth extends to back of eye; jaws even	mouth extends to middle of eye	mouth extends to middle of eye	mouth below snout

Clupeidae

AMERICAN SHAD

Alosa sapidissima

Other Names: river, silver or white shad

Habitat: coastal marine most of the year; migrates up large rivers to spawn; landlocked in a few areas

Range: the Atlantic coast and spawning rivers from Newfoundland to Florida; coastal rivers in the Carolinas

Food: plankton, crustaceans, small fish

Reproduction: American Shad migrate upstream when water temperature reaches 62 to 67 degrees; spawning takes place in large rivers at the mouth of tributary streams; in the north, adults return to the sea after spawning; in the south, adults often die after spawning

Average Size: 18 to 20 inches, 2 to 3 pounds

Records: NC—7 pounds, 15 ounces, Tar River, 1974; SC—7 pounds, Santee River, 1994; North American—11 pounds, 4 ounces, Connecticut River, Massachusetts, 1986

Notes: The American Shad is a large shad similar to the Hickory Shad and spawns in the same Carolina waters at about the same time. Like other shad, the American Shad makes a spring spawning run; in fact, the American Shad helped save George Washington's starving troops at Valley Forge. Today, the spring run is still an important commercial and sport-fishing event in the Carolinas. American Shad readily take small artificial lures and have become very popular with fly fishermen. Shad are oily fish that are very good when smoked, baked or fried. Many Carolinians also prize shad roe.

Description: deep, laterally compressed silver body with blue back; one dark spot on the shoulder just behind the gill; sawtooth edge of sharply pointed scales along the belly (scutes); black lining in body cavity (silver in the Alewife)

Similar Species: Alewife (pg. 48), American Shad (pg. 50), Blueback Herring (pg. 52), Gizzard Shad (pg. 54)

Blueback Herring

black body cavity lining; mouth extends to middle of eye; underbite

Alewife

silver-gray body cavity lining

American Shad

mouth extends to back of eye

Gizzard Shad

mouth below snout

Clupeidae

BLUEBACK HERRING

Alosa aestivalis

Other Names: glut herring

Habitat: coastal marine most of the year; migrates up rivers and streams to spawn

Range: the Atlantic coast from Nova Scotia to the St. Johns River, Florida and associated spawning rivers; Carolina coastal waters and a few inland reservoirs in NC

Food: marine plankton feeders

Reproduction: Blueback Herring are "anadromous" and live in salt water but spawn in fresh water; they migrate to brackish river mouths or upstream to spawn when water temperatures are near 57 degrees; they have an extended spawning season that lasts 3 months; eggs are deposited in moving water over sand or gravel

Average Size: 10 to 12 inches, 12 ounces

Records: none

Notes: The Blueback Herring is closely related to the Alewife and is sometimes found in mixed migrating schools, though each species prefers different spawning habitats. Bluebacks spawn in faster, warmer water with a firmer substrate than that preferred by the Alewife. Bluebacks may migrate far upstream or spawn in brackish water. Due to their great numbers at stream mouths during spawning season, the Blueback Herring have acquired the name "glut herring."

Description: deep, laterally compressed body; silvery-blue back with white sides and belly; young fish have a dark spot on shoulder behind the gill; small mouth; last rays of dorsal fin form a long thread

Similar Species: Alewife (pg. 48), American Shad (pg. 50), Blueback Herring (pg. 52)

Gizzard Shad	Alewife	American Shad	Blueback Herring
mouth below snout	mouth not below snout	jaws even	underbite

GIZZARD SHAD

Dorosoma cepedianum

Other Names: hickory, mud or jack shad

Habitat: large rivers, reservoirs, lakes, swamps and temporarily flooded pools; brackish and saline waters in coastal areas

Range: the St. Lawrence, Great Lakes, Mississippi, Atlantic and Gulf Slope drainages from Quebec to Mexico, south to central Florida; common throughout the Carolinas

Food: herbivorous filter feeder

Reproduction: spawning takes place in tributary streams and along lakeshores in early summer; schooling adults release eggs in open water without regard to mates

Average Size: 6 to 8 inches, 1 to 8 ounces

Records: NC—none; SC—none; North American—4 pounds, 12 ounces, Lake Oahe, South Dakota, 2006

Notes: The Gizzard Shad is a widespread, prolific fish that is best known as forage for popular game fish. It can overpopulate some reservoirs and become the dominant species, growing too large to be prey. The name "gizzard" refers to this shad's long, convoluted intestine that is often packed with sand. Though Gizzard Shad are a management problem at times, they form a valuable link in turning plankton into usable forage for larger game fish. Occasionally, larger Gizzard Shad are caught with hook and line, but they have little food value.

Description: deep, laterally compressed silver body; dark olive back; several spots on shoulder behind the gill; head and cheeks bronze; sharply pointed scales along belly; more angular appearance than other shad.

Similar Species: Alewife (pg. 48), American Shad (pg. 50), Gizzard Shad (pg. 54), Blueback Herring (pg. 52)

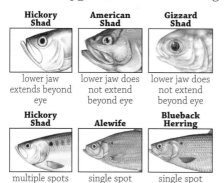

Hickory Shad	American Shad	Gizzard Shad
lower jaw extends beyond eye	lower jaw does not extend beyond eye	lower jaw does not extend beyond eye

Hickory Shad	Alewife	Blueback Herring
multiple spots behind gill	single spot behind gill	single spot behind gill

HICKORY SHAD
Alosa mediocris

Other Names: silver or bronze shad

Habitat: coastal marine most of the year; migrates up rivers and streams to spawn

Range: Atlantic coast from Maine to the St. Johns River, Florida and associated spawning rivers; coastal Carolina rivers

Food: marine plankton feeders

Reproduction: Hickory Shad are "anadromous," and migrate to fresh water to spawn; spawning takes place at night when water temperatures reach 61 degrees; buoyant eggs are released and drift downstream with the current

Average Size: 10 to 14 inches, 1 pound to 1 pound, 8 ounces

Records: NC—4 pounds, 1 ounce, Pitchkettle Creek; SC—none; North American—2 pounds, 8 ounces, James River, Virginia, 2006 (IGFA)

Notes: The Hickory Shad and the American Shad are the two large shad species that enter the coastal streams of the Carolinas in the spring. Unlike American Shad, which prefer the main river currents, Hickory Shad prefer spawning in small tributary streams. The Hickory Shad is prized by light tackle anglers for its strong fighting ability and high leaps when hooked. However, Hickory Shad are not as meaty as American Shad and not as popular for the table.

SEA LAMPREY

MOUNTAIN BROOK LAMPREY

Description: eel-like body; round sucking-disk mouth; seven paired gill openings; long dorsal fin connects with tail; no paired fins; Sea Lamprey—dorsal fin divided; Mountain Brook Lamprey—unnotched dorsal fin

Similar Species: American Eel (pg. 44)

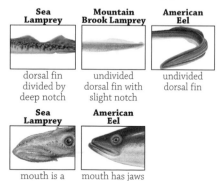

Sea Lamprey	Mountain Brook Lamprey	American Eel
dorsal fin divided by deep notch	undivided dorsal fin with slight notch	undivided dorsal fin

Sea Lamprey	American Eel
mouth is a sucking disk	mouth has jaws

SEA LAMPREY *Petromyzon marinus*

Petromyzontidae

MOUNTAIN BROOK LAMPREY *Ichthyomyzon greeleyi*

Other Names: Mountain Brook—river or freshwater lamprey; Sea—lake or ocean lamprey

Habitat: Mountain—juveniles live in quiet pools of streams and rivers; some adults may move into lakes; Sea—juveniles live in streams and rivers, adults in coastal marine waters

Range: Mountain—fresh waters of eastern U.S.; tributaries of the upper Tennessee River in NC; Sea—the Atlantic Ocean and the Great Lakes; coastal streams and marine waters of NC and SC

Food: juvenile lampreys are bottom filter feeders in freshwater streams; adult Sea Lampreys are parasitic on fish; adult Brook Lampreys do not feed

Reproduction: adult lampreys build a nest in the gravel of streambeds when water temperature reaches the mid-50s; adults die soon after spawning

Average Size: Mountain—6 to 12 inches; Sea—12 to 24 inches

Records: none

Notes: Lampreys are some of earth's oldest vertebrates, with fossil records dating back 500 million years. These primitive fish have skeletons made of cartilage. All lampreys spawn in freshwater. Both lamprey species are native to the Carolinas and coexist with other fish species with little or no harmful effects. Due to deteriorating water conditions, many stream lampreys are endangered or threatened throughout their range.

SOUTHERN FLOUNDER

SUMMER FLOUNDER

Description: side with eyes is light to dark brown with dark spots and blotches that do not have dark centers; light brown mottled fins; side without eyes is creamy white without spots; flat flounder-like body with eyes on top

Similar Species: Hogchoker (pg. 114)

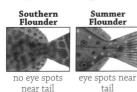

Southern Flounder	Summer Flounder
no eye spots near tail	eye spots near tail

Flounders	Hogchoker
dorsal and anal fins extends to head	dorsal fin extends to mouth

SOUTHERN FLOUNDER
Paralichthys lethostigma

SUMMER FLOUNDER
Paralichthys dentatus

Bothidae

Other Names: mud flounder, doormat, halibut

Habitat: marine areas; migrates up freshwater rivers; prefers water with a sand or silt bottom

Range: the Atlantic coast from North Carolina to Mexico, the Gulf Coast from Florida to Texas; common in the larger coastal rivers of the Carolinas

Food: small fish

Reproduction: adults migrate offshore to spawn in late fall

Average Size: 12 to 24 inches; 2 to 6 pounds

Records: state—none; North American—20 pounds, 9 ounces, Nassau Sound, Florida, 1982 (IGFA)

Notes: Flounders primarily inhabit the open ocean and estuaries, but many migrate into large freshwater rivers during the summer. Flounders are a common catch in the lower reaches of coastal rivers, but fishermen are often surprised when they catch one many miles from the ocean. Young flounders swim upright with an eye on each side; as they mature, one eye migrates, some to the left side and some to the right side. Southern Flounders belong to the family of left eye flounders and the fish lie on their right side at maturity. The Summer Flounder is also very common in the Carolinas and can be distinguished by the 5 "eye" spots that form near the tail.

61

Description: silver to olive green back and sides; scales out-lined, giving sides a cross-hatched appearance; upturned mouth; dark bar under eye; rounded tail fin

Similar Species: Brook Silverside (pg. 110), Lined Topminnow (pg. 170)

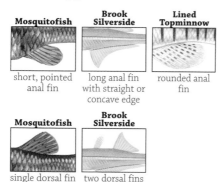

Mosquitofish	**Brook Silverside**	**Lined Topminnow**
short, pointed anal fin	long anal fin with straight or concave edge	rounded anal fin

Mosquitofish	**Brook Silverside**
single dorsal fin	two dorsal fins

MOSQUITOFISH

Gambusia holbrooki

Other Names: mosquito or surface minnow

Habitat: surface of shallow, well-vegetated backwaters with little current; lakes and swamps

Range: the southeastern U.S, introduced worldwide; common in the Carolinas, except in the far west

Food: insects, crustaceans and some plant material

Reproduction: gives birth to live young after internal fertilization; may produce several broods in a single season

Average Size: 2 to 3 inches

Records: none

Notes: There are few native livebearers in the U.S., but it is a well represented family in the tropical and subtropical Americas. Male Mosquitofish use their modified anal fin to transfer sperm to the much larger females. Females can then store the sperm for up to ten months. Mosquitofish have been introduced worldwide to control mosquitoes but seem to be no better at it than native species. Mosquitofish are hardy and can tolerate high temperatures, high salinity and low oxygen levels and can therefore be found in almost any quiet body of water.

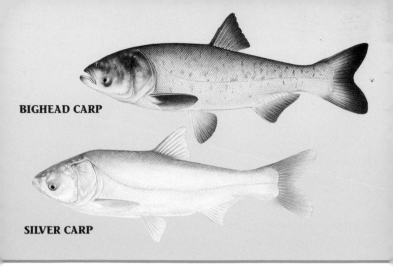

BIGHEAD CARP

SILVER CARP

Description: large body; upturned mouth without barbels; low set eyes; small body scales; no scales on head

Similar Species: Common Carp (pg. 66), Grass Carp (pg. 68)

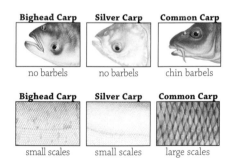

Bighead Carp	Silver Carp	Common Carp
no barbels	no barbels	chin barbels

Bighead Carp	Silver Carp	Common Carp
small scales	small scales	large scales

BIGHEAD CARP
"Hypophthalmichthys nobils

Cyprinidae

SILVER CARP Hypophthalmichthys molitrix

Species Names: Silver— shiner carp; Bighead—river carp, lake fish, speckled amur

Habitat: large, warm rivers and connected lakes

Range: native to Asia, introduced in other parts of the world; in the Carolinas, both species are restricted to aquaculture ponds

Food: plankton, algae

Reproduction: spawns from late spring to early summer in warm, flowing water

Average Size: 16 to 22 inches, 5 to 50 pounds

Records: NC—none; SC—none; North American—Bighead Carp, 90 pounds, Kirby Lake, Texas, 2000

Notes: Bighead and Silver Carp were introduced into the United States to control unwanted species in southern aquaculture ponds. They are important fish and farmed for food in many other countries. Both species have escaped from ponds in Arkansas to become established in the Mississippi, Ohio and Illinois Rivers with devastating effect. Both species are voracious feeders that have the potential to disrupt the entire food web, but these two species are not currently a problem in the Carolinas. The Silver Carp, and to a lesser extent the Bighead Carp, makes high leaps from the water when frightened by boats.

65

Description: brassy yellow to golden brown or dark olive back and sides; white to yellow belly; two pairs of barbels near round, extendable mouth; red-tinged tail and anal fin; each scale has a dark spot at base and a dark margin

Similar Species: Bighead Carp (pg. 64), Grass Carp (pg. 68), Silver Carp (pg. 64)

Common Carp	**Bighead Carp**	**Grass Carp**	**Silver Carp**
downturned mouth with barbels	upturned mouth lacks barbels, eyes low on head	mouth upturned, no barbels, eye low on head	upturned mouth lacks barbels, eyes low on head

COMMON CARP

Cyprinus carpio

Other Names: German, European, mirror or leather carp, buglemouth

Habitat: warm, shallow, quiet, weedy waters of streams and lakes

Range: native to Asia, introduced worldwide; common throughout the Carolinas

Food: opportunistic feeder, prefers insect larvae, crustaceans and mollusks, but will eat algae and some higher plants

Reproduction: spawns from late spring to early summer in very shallow water at stream and lake edges; very obvious when spawning with a great deal of splashing

Average Size: 16 to 18 inches, 5 to 20 pounds

Records: NC—48 pounds, Mecklenburg County Pond, 1986; SC—none; North American—57 pounds, 13 ounces, Tidal Basin, Washington D.C., 1983

Notes: One of the world's most important freshwater species, the fast-growing Common Carp provides sport and food for millions of people throughout its range. This Asian minnow was introduced into Europe in the twelfth century but didn't make it to North America until the 1800s. Carp are a highly prized sport fish in Europe but are generally disliked in the U.S., even though Carp taken from clean water have a fine flavor. The meat is oily and bony and is best prepared when soaked in a sweet brine and then smoked.

Description: silver-gray head and sides with a golden green sheen; fins grayish-green; large scales; eye set in middle of head; terminal mouth; torpedo-shaped body not as deep as common carp

Similar Species: Common Carp (pg. 66)

Grass Carp	Common Carp
moth upturned, no barbels, eye low on head	downturned mouth with barbels, eye high on head

GRASS CARP

Ctenopharyngodon idella

Cyprinidae

Other Names: white amur, silver or weed carp

Habitat: warm, shallow, quiet weedy waters of streams and lakes

Range: native to Siberia's lower Amur River and northern China, now established in 20 countries; uncommon but found throughout the Carolinas

Food: aquatic vegetation

Reproduction: spawn in streams where eggs are released and fertilized in a slow current; only stocked as non-reproducing sterile fish

Average Size: 24 to 30 inches, 5 to 20 pounds

Records: NC—68 pounds, 12 ounces, Summerlins Pond, 1998; SC—none; North American—80 pounds, Lake Wedington, Arkansas, 2004 IGFA

Notes: Grass Carp were first brought to the United States in 1961 by the U.S. Fish and Wildlife Service to control aquatic vegetation. It was soon learned that by exposing the eggs to heat, sterile fish could be produced. These triploid fish (fish with three sets of chromosomes instead of the normal two) are now stocked in the Carolinas in order to control aquatic vegetation and there are always a few escapees. Grass Carp do not take bait readily, but a few are caught by anglers and are often large enough to put up a great fight. All hooked fish should be released so they can go about their job of weed control.

Description: dark olive back; iridescent purple or silver sides; white belly; dark spot at base of dorsal fin

Similar Species: Golden Shiner (pg. 76)

Creek Chub	Golden Shiner	Creek Chub	Golden Shiner
mouth large, extends to eye	small mouth barely extends to eye	rounded anal fin, 7 to 9 rays	angular anal fin, 11 to 15 rays

CREEK CHUB

Semotilus atromaculatus

Other Names: common, brook, silver, mud or blackspot chub, horned or northern horned dace

Habitat: primarily found in quiet pools in clear streams and rivers; occasionally in lakes

Range: Montana southward through the Gulf States; common in the Carolinas except the coastal plains

Food: small aquatic invertebrates and crustaceans

Reproduction: in late spring, male excavates a 1- to 3-foot-long, teardrop-shaped pit at the head of stream riffles by using its mouth or rolling stones with its head; the pits are filled until 6 to 8 inches high; females lay eggs on the mound, which are then covered and defended by the male; several other minnow species may spawn on the mound, occasionally resulting in hybridization

Average Size: 4 to 10 inches, up to 6 ounces

Records: none

Notes: The Creek Chub is one of the most common stream fishes in eastern North America. They take bait readily and are often fished for by young children spending a day on the creek. When water levels are low in late summer, the chub spawning mounds can be plentiful and quite evident, leaving many to speculate on their origin. Chubs are a highly prized bait minnow, and local populations can be easily depleted by overharvesting.

Description: reddish-olive mottled back and sides; faint dark stripe on sides from head to tail; long, pointy nose; very small scales

Similar Species: Eastern Mudminnow (pg. 78)

Longnose Dace	Eastern Mudminnow	Longnose Dace	Eastern Mudminnow
long, pointed pectoral fins	short, rounded pectoral fin	angular dorsal and anal fins deep notched tail fin	rounded dorsal, tail and anal fin

LONGNOSE DACE

Rhinichthys cataractae

Cyprinidae

Other Names: Great Lakes dace, leatherback, stream shooter

Habitat: small and medium-sized streams with strong currents; windy, rocky shorelines of large lakes

Range: Northwest Territories to Hudson Bay, the northeastern U.S. and eastern Canada; western mountainous parts of the Carolinas

Food: primarily zooplankton, aquatic insects

Reproduction: spawns in the fast current at the base of riffles when water temperature reaches the low 60s; males defend a spawning site and attack intruders; females lay a few hundred to a thousand adhesive eggs; no parental care

Average Size: 2 to 3 inches

Records: none

Notes: A small group of minnows in the Carolinas are referred to as daces. They are small fish that live in a variety of habitats. The Longnose Dace is a brightly colored, strong swimmer that is often found in the active water of fast streams or beach surf. They are hardy fish that can withstand rapid environmental changes and do well in aquariums with cool water. Often found in large schools when streams are low, the Longnose Dace can be very susceptible to overharvesting for bait

Description: olive yellow-brown back; silver sides with a faint dark stripe along lateral line; rounded snout and fins; scales are outlined with a cross-hatched appeerence; dark blotch on front of dorsal fin and dark spot at base of tail fin

Similar Species: Creek Chub (pg. 70)

Bluntnose Minnow

small down-turned mouth

Creek Chub

mouth large and terminal

Bluntnose Minnow

first dorsal ray short, split from others

Creek Chub

first dorsal ray not split from others

BLUNTNOSE MINNOW

Cyprinidae

Pimephales notatus

Other Names: spot tail minnow, tuffy

Habitat: shallow pools of small to midsized streams; shallow, weedy lakes and ponds

Range: central U.S. from the Gulf to the Great Lakes; north-western North Carolina

Food: insects and copepods

Reproduction: males prepare a nest beneath rocks and sticks; females enter nest and turn upside down to lay adhesive eggs on an overhang; male fans the eggs and massages them with a special mucus-like pad on its back

Average Size: 3 to 4 inches

Records: none

Notes: There are over 1500 minnow species in the world, with 200 present in North America and 50 species found in the Carolinas. The Bluntnose Minnow is a common bait pail minnow and is farmed throughout the Carolinas. Without question, it is one of the most economically important fish in the U.S. Though its range barely extends into North Carolina, small populations can be expected anywhere in the Carolinas because of escapees or accidental releases.

Description: back gold to greenish gold; sides golden with silver reflections; belly yellowish silver; deep slab sided body; mouth angled up; long, triangular head

Similar Species: Creek Chub (pg. 70)

Golden Shiner	**Creek Chub**	**Golden Shiner**	**Creek Chub**
mouth is small and barely extends to eye	mouth is large and extends to eye	angular anal fin, 11 to 15 rays	rounded anal fin, 7 to 9 rays

GOLDEN SHINER

Cyprinidae

Notemigonus crysoleucas

Other Names: bream, American bream, roach, American roach, butterfish, pond shiner

Habitat: clear, weedy ponds and quiet streams

Range: native to the eastern U.S. and south to Florida, introduced in the West; common throughout the Carolinas

Food: planktonic crustaceans, aquatic insects, mollusks

Reproduction: extended midsummer spawning season; a female, attended by one or two males, spreads adhesive eggs over submerged vegetation; no parental care

Average Size: 3 to 7 inches

Records: none

Notes: Many of the Carolina minnows are called shiners; most are in the genus *Notropis*. Not all shiners are as flashy as the name indicates; some are dull and show almost no silver or gold on the sides. The Golden Shiner lives up to the name. It is a large, showy minnow that congregates in large schools, particularly when young. It is sometimes found in open water, but never far from vegetation. Golden Shiners are an important forage and baitfish; small ones are prized as bait for panfish, large ones as bait for bass. They are commonly seined from the wild or propagated in fertilized ponds.

77

Description: olive green back; tan to yellow-brown sides with faint, wavy vertical bars; rounded tail fin; dark bar just before the tail; slightly flattened head

Similar Species: Longnose Dace (pg. 72)

Eastern Mudminnow	Longnose Dace	Eastern Mudminnow	Longnose Dace
short, rounded pectoral fin	long, pointed pectoral fins	rounded dorsal, tail and anal fin	angular dorsal and anal fins; deeply notched tail fin

EASTERN MUDMINNOW

Umbra pygmaea

Other Names: coastal mudminnow, dogfish, mudfish

Habitat: slow, stagnant waters of weedy streams and ponds with soft bottoms

Range: Atlantic states from New York to northern Florida; lower piedmont and coastal plains of the Carolinas

Food: insects, mollusks, and larger crustaceans

Reproduction: in the early spring, adults move into flooded pools when water temperatures reach the mid-50s; yellow-orange eggs are deposited singly on plant leaves and are left to hatch without parental care

Average Size: 3 inches

Records: none

Notes: This hardy little fish can withstand very low oxygen levels as it can gulp air to breathe when necessary (even from air bubbles under the ice). Eastern Mudminnows hide in the bottom detritus but do not bury themselves tail first in the mud, as often reported. They are frequently the only fish left after ponds dry up and are depleted of oxygen. Not surprisingly, they are a good baitfish, withstanding the bait pail and hooks well. They can be fun aquarium fish and quickly learn to eat small pieces of meat or angle worms when offered.

79

Description: pale brown to sandy back and sides; sides are "tessellated" and have a mosaic-like checkered pattern; markings become more pronounced and colors brighter on breeding males

Similar Species: Mottled Sculpin (pg. 108)

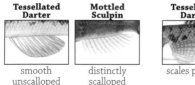

Tessellated Darter	Mottled Sculpin
smooth unscalloped anal fin	distinctly scalloped anal fin

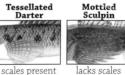

Tessellated Darter	Mottled Sculpin
scales present	lacks scales

TESSELLATED DARTER

Etheostoma olmstedi

Percidae

Other Names: red-sided, yellowbelly, or weed darter

Habitat: the bottom of sandy, muddy pools of headwaters, creeks and small to medium rivers; lakeshore

Range: the Atlantic slope from the St. Lawrence River in Quebec to the St. Johns river in Florida; from upper Piedmont through coastal plains in the Carolinas

Food: small aquatic invertebrates

Reproduction: in May and June, males migrate to shorelines or current edges to establish breeding areas; females move from territory to territory, spawning with several males; each sequence produces 7 to 10 eggs which attach to the bottom

Average Size: 2 to 4 inches

Records: none

Notes: A relative of the Yellow Perch and Walleye, the Tessellated Darter is primarily a stream fish and has adapted to living among the rocks in fast current. A small swim bladder allows darters to sink rapidly to the bottom after a "dart," thereby avoiding being swept away by the current. Darters are hard to see when they move, but are easy to spot when perched on their pectoral fins. The Carolinas have a large number of darter species, many with restricted ranges. The Tessellated Darter is primarily a stream species but can be found in a wide range of habitats. Darters are good aquarium fish but require some live food.

81

Description: slender body; gray to dark silver or yellowish-brown with dark blotches on sides; black spots on spiny dorsal fin; may exhibit some white on lower margin of tail, but lacks the prominent white spot found on Walleye

Similar Species: Walleye (pg. 84)

Sauger	Walleye	Sauger	Walleye
spiny dorsal fin is spotted, lacks dark blotch on rear base	spiny dorsal fin lacks spots, large dark blotch on rear base	blotches on sides below lateral line	lacks blotches on sides below lateral line

SAUGER

Sander canadensis

Percidae

Other Names: sand pike, spotfin pike, river pike, jackfish, jack salmon

Habitat: large lakes and rivers

Range: large lakes in southern Canada, the northern U.S. and the wider reaches of the Mississippi, Missouri, Ohio and Tennessee River drainages; introduced to streams and reservoirs in the far western Carolinas

Food: small fish, aquatic insects, crayfish

Reproduction: spawns in April and May as water approaches 50 degrees; adults move into the shallow waters of tributaries and headwaters to randomly deposit eggs over gravel beds

Average Size: 10 to 12 inches, 8 ounces to 2 pounds

Records: NC—5 pounds, 15 ounces, Norman Lake, 1971; SC—4 pounds, 7 ounces, Lake Thurmond, 1985; North American—8 pounds, 12 ounces, Lake Sakakawea, North Dakota, 1971

Notes: Though the Sauger is the Walleye's smaller cousin, it is a big water fish, residing primarily in large lakes and rivers. It grows slowly, and only reaches two pounds after twenty years in very cold water. The Sauger is native to the Tennessee drainage but was not originally found east of the Appalachians. It is an aggressive daytime feeder when compared to Walleye, but is still more productively fished in the evenings, early mornings and at night. Its fine, flavored flesh is top table fare.

83

Description: long, round body; dark silver or golden to dark olive brown sides; spines in both first dorsal and anal fin; sharp canine teeth; dark spot at base of the three last spines of the dorsal fin; white spot on bottom lobe of tail

Similar Species: Sauger (pg. 82)

Walleye	Sauger	Walleye	Sauger
spiny dorsal fin lacks spots, large dark blotch on rear base	spiny dorsal fin is spotted, lacks dark blotch on rear base	lacks blotches on sides below lateral line	blotches on sides below lateral line

WALLEYE

Sander vitreus

Percidae

Other Names: marble-eyes, walleyed pike, jack, jackfish, Susquehanna salmon

Habitat: lakes and streams, abundant in very large lakes

Range: originally the northern states and Canada, now widely stocked throughout the U.S.; commonly stocked in the Piedmont and mountain regions of the Carolinas

Food: small fish, insects, crayfish, leeches

Reproduction: spawns in tributary streams or rocky lake shoals when spring water temperatures reach 45 to 50 degrees; no parental care

Average Size: 14 to 17 inches, 1 to 3 pounds

Records: NC—13 pounds, 8 ounces, Lake Chatuge, 1986; SC—10 pounds, Lake Russell, 1994; North American—21 pounds, 11 ounces, Greer's Ferry Lake, Arkansas, 1982

Notes: The Walleye is a popular sport fish, and while not a great fighter, it is a dogged opponent. The Walleye is not native to the Carolinas; it was one of the first game fish introduced to the region and is now the favorite of many anglers. Its mild-flavored flesh is considered by many to be the best eating of all freshwater fish. A reflective layer of pigment in the eye allows Walleyes to see in low light conditions, and they are most active during low light conditions, under cloudy skies, at dusk, dawn or through the night. Walleyes are a coldwater fish and are only found in the shallows when the water is very cool.

85

Description: 6 to 9 olive green vertical bars on a yellow-brown background; two separate dorsal fins, the front all spines, the back soft rays; lower fins tinged yellow or orange, brighter in breeding males

Similar Species: Sauger (pg. 82), Walleye (pg. 84)

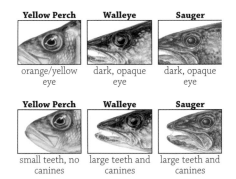

Yellow Perch	Walleye	Sauger
orange/yellow eye	dark, opaque eye	dark, opaque eye

Yellow Perch	Walleye	Sauger
small teeth, no canines	large teeth and canines	large teeth and canines

YELLOW PERCH

Perca flavescens

Other Names: ringed, striped or jack perch, green hornet

Habitat: lakes and streams, prefers clear, open water

Range: widely introduced throughout southern Canada and the northern U.S.; common in the Carolinas except southern South Carolina

Food: prefers minnows, insects, snails, leeches and crayfish

Reproduction: spawns at night in shallow, weedy areas when water temperatures reach 45 degrees; females drape gelatinous ribbons of eggs on submerged vegetation

Average Size: 8 to 11 inches, 6 to 10 ounces

Records: NC—none; SC—3 pounds, 4 ounces, Lake Keowee, 1979; North American—4 pounds, 3 ounces, Bordentown, New Jersey, 1865

Notes: The Yellow Perch is very common throughout much of the United States and has been introduced far beyond its native range. Over much of its range, it is a popular pan-fish; there is even a commercial fishery in the Great Lakes. In the Carolinas, Yellow Perch can be very abundant, but are often stunted and quite small. Even though few anglers in the Carolinas target them, Perch that are large enough to keep have firm, white flesh and are excellent table fare. Many anglers in northern states rank Yellow Perch alongside Walleye in terms of flavor.

Description: olive green to yellow-brown back and sides; yellow-green chain-like markings on the sides; distinct dark teardrop below the eye; scales on the entire cheek and gill covers; fins almost clear

Similar Species: Redfin Pickerel (pg. 90), Northern Pike (pg. 94)

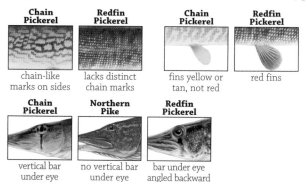

Chain Pickerel	**Redfin Pickerel**		**Chain Pickerel**	**Redfin Pickerel**
chain-like marks on sides	lacks distinct chain marks		fins yellow or tan, not red	red fins

Chain Pickerel	**Northern Pike**	**Redfin Pickerel**
vertical bar under eye	no vertical bar under eye	bar under eye angled backward

CHAIN PICKEREL

Esox niger

Esocidae

Other Names: weed, jack or chain pike, jack pickerel

Habitat: shallow, weedy lakes and sluggish streams

Range: eastern United States from the Great Lakes and Maine to Florida and west through the Gulf States to Texas; common in the Piedmont and coastal plains of the Carolinas

Food: small fish, aquatic invertebrates

Reproduction: spawning takes place in April and May just as the ice goes out; adhesive eggs are deposited over shallow submerged vegetation and left to hatch with no parental care; occasionally spawns in fall with very low survival rate

Average Size: 18 to 24 inches, 1 to 3 pounds

Records: NC—8 pounds, Gaston Reservoir, 1968; SC—6 pounds, 4 ounces, Chessey Creek, 1981; North American—9 pounds, 6 ounces, Homerville, Georgia, 1961

Notes: The Chain Pickerel is the largest of the pickerels and a respected game fish. Chain Pickerels frequent the outside edges of weedbeds and bite readily on minnow imitation lures. When fished on light tackle or a fly rod, they put up a good fight. Chain Pickerels have a tendency to stunt when overpopulated, filling lakes and channels with half-pound "hammer handles." All members of the pike family have intramuscular "Y" bones, an adaptation which enables them to lunge suddenly and capture prey. The Chain Pickerel's flesh is flavorful, but their small "Y" bones make them unpopular as table fare.

Description: olive green to yellow-brown back and sides; sides have worm-like bars; distinct dark teardrop below eye; lower fins are tinged red, bright red in breeding males; scales on the entire cheek and gill cover

Similar Species: Chain Pickerel (pg. 88); Northern Pike (pg. 94)

Redfin Pickerel	**Northern Pike**		**Redfin Pickerel**	**Chain Pickerel**
bar under eye	no bar under eye		red fins	fins yellow or tan, not red

Redfin Pickerel	**Chain Pickerel**
lacks distinct chain marks	chain-like marks on sides

REDFIN PICKEREL

Esox americanus americanus

Esocidae

Other Names: red, mud, banded or little pickerel, red, grass, red-finned or mud pike

Habitat: shallow, weedy lakes and sluggish streams

Range: Atlantic states from Maine to Florida (east of the Alleghenies) and east through the Gulf States; common in the coastal plains of the Carolinas, uncommon in the Piedmont

Food: small fish, aquatic invertebrates

Reproduction: spawns in early spring just as the ice goes out; adults enter flooded meadows and shallow bays and lay eggs in less than 2 feet of water; adhesive eggs are deposited over shallow, submerged vegetation; eggs are left to hatch with no parental care; similar spawning biology results in occasional hybridization with Chain Pickerel

Average Size: 10 to 12 inches, under 1 pound

Records: NC—2 pounds, 4 ounces, Gallberry Lake, 1997; SC—1 pound, 8.8 ounces, Bluff Lake, 1983; North American—2 pounds, 10 ounces, Lewis Lake, Georgia, 1982

Notes: The Redfin Pickerel is the smallest member of the pike family and is a common fish in weedy lakes and streams along the Atlantic seaboard. Redfin Pickerels are scrappy fighters on light tackle, but, due to their small size, are little more than a nuisance to panfish anglers. Redfin Pickerel eat some small fish but their diet consists largely of invertebrates, including crayfish.

91

MUSKELLUNGE

TIGER MUSKIE

Description: torpedo-shaped body; dorsal fin near tail; dark
gray-green back; silver to silver-green sides; dark vertical
bars or blotches on sides (dark markings on light background); pointed tail; no scales on lower half of gill covers

Similar Species: Redfin Pickerel (pg. 90), Chain Pickerel
(pg. 88), Northern Pike (pg. 94)

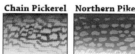

Muskellunge	Chain Pickerel	Northern Pike
dark marks on light background	chain-like marks on sides	light marks on dark background

Muskellunge	Northern Pike	Tiger Muskie
pointed tail	rounded tail	rounded tail

MUSKELLUNGE

Esox masquinongy

Other Names: Great Lakes or Ohio Muskellunge, muskie, northern, 'ski, lunge

Habitat: waters of large, clear, weedy lakes; medium to large rivers with slow currents and deep pools

Range: the Great Lakes basin east to Maine, south through the Ohio River drainage to Tennessee; native in the Little Tennessee River system and stocked (along with Tiger Muskies) in a few western Carolina lakes and streams

Food: small fish, occasionally baby muskrats, ducklings

Reproduction: spawning takes place in late spring when water temperatures reach 50 to 60 degrees; eggs are laid in dead vegetation in streams or bays with a soft bottom

Average Size: 30 to 42 inches, 10 to 20 pounds

Records: NC—41 pounds, 8 ounces, Lake Adger, 2001; SC—22 pounds, 8 ounces, Broad River, 2004; North American—69 pounds, 11 ounces, Chippewa Flowage, Wisconsin, 1949

Notes: The Muskellunge is the prize of all freshwater game fishing. This big, fast predator prefers large, shallow, clear lakes or rivers with quiet pools. Muskies are rare to uncommon over most of their range; typically, there is one fish every two to three acres. They are hard to entice with lures or bait and musky fishermen average over 50 hours of fishing before catching a legal fish. Muskellunge readily hybridize with Northern Pike, producing Tiger Muskellunge and pure musky stock is rare. Tiger Muskellunge are easier to rear and preferred for many stocking programs.

93

Description: elongated body with dorsal fin near tail; head long and flattened in front, forming a duck-like snout; dark green back; light green sides with bean-shaped light spots (light markings on dark background)

Similar Species: Muskellunge (pg. 92), Tiger Muskie (pg. 92), Chain Pickerel (pg. 88)

Northern Pike	**Chain Pickerel**	**Muskellunge**	**Tiger Muskie**
light spots on dark background	chain-like marks on sides	dark marks on light background	dark marks on light background

Northern Pike	**Muskellunge**
rounded tail	pointed tail

NORTHERN PIKE

Esox lucius

Other Names: northern, pickerel or great northern pickerel, jack or jackfish, hammer handle, snot rocket

Habitat: lakes and slow-moving streams often associated with vegetation

Range: northern Europe, Asia, and North America; stocked in a few lakes in North Carolina

Food: small fish, frogs, crayfish

Reproduction: in early spring as water temperature reaches 34 to 40 degrees; eggs are laid among shallow vegetation in tributary streams and near lake edges; no parental care

Average Size: 18 to 24 inches, 2 to 5 pounds

Records: NC—11 pounds, 13 ounces, Lake James, 1978; SC —none; North American—46 pounds, 2 ounces, Great Sacandaga Lake, New York, 1940

Notes: This large, fast predator is one of the most widespread freshwater fish in the world and a prime sport fish throughout its range. Its long, tube-shaped body and intramuscular bones are adaptations for quick bursts of speed. Pike are sight-feeders and hunt by lying in wait and capturing their prey with a lighting-fast lunge. Many anglers have lost their catch just at the boat when the pike employed this burst of speed to escape. The Tiger Muskie is the Northern Pike-Muskellunge hybrid and is considered a Muskie in bag limits.

Description: dark green to gray-green back; lower sides dark tan with black specks; body has an overall purple sheen; dark bar at base of tail; single dorsal fin; big mouth and head; anus just below gills

Similar Species: Green Sunfish (pg. 148)

Pirate Perch	Green Sunfish	Pirate Perch	Green Sunfish
protruding lower jaw	jaws almost even	rounded, front portion of dorsal fin	long, spiny portion of dorsal fin

Pirate Perch	Green Sunfish
rounded tail, bar at base	slightly forked tail, no bar

PIRATE PERCH
Aphredoderus sayanus

Aphredoderidae

Other Names: green perch

Habitat: low gradient streams and creeks, swamps, ponds and roadside ditches, all with a soft bottom and thick vegetation

Range: the Mississippi drainage to the Great Lakes; the Gulf and Atlantic states; common in the Carolina coastal plains

Food: insects, crustaceans, small fish

Reproduction: from early spring through summer, both adults build a nest then guard eggs and young

Average Size: 2 to 5 inches

Records: none

Notes: Pirate Perch are small, secretive fish that hide during the day in thick aquatic vegetation or bottom debris. They aggressively feed on insects during the early morning, late evening and at night. In juvenile fish, the anus is near the anal fins, but it migrates to the gill area as the fish matures. In other species, this trait is associated with eggs which are brooded under the gills; however, gill brooding has not been observed in Pirate Perch. Pirate Perch were named for their propensity to attack and kill other fish when kept in an aquarium. A few anglers feel this hardy little fish is superior to other baitfish and go to great lengths to obtain them.

Description: dark olive green-brown body and head covered with black specks; 10 or 11 black bands on sides; black bands on dorsal, anal and tail fins; sunfish shape with rounded fins

Similar Species: Eastern Mudminnow (pg. 78), Lined Topminnow (pg. 170)

Banded Pygmy Sunfish	Eastern Mudminnow	Lined Topminnow
terminal mouth, large eye	terminal mouth, small eye	upturned mouth

Banded Pygmy Sunfish	Eastern Mudminnow	Lined Topminnow
hard and soft rays are large	soft rays large	soft rays small

BANDED PYGMY SUNFISH

Elassoma zanatum

Elassomatidae

Other Names: little banded sunfish

Habitat: lakes, creeks and coastal swamps that are heavily vegetated with quiet waters and a soft bottom

Range: southeastern states from North Carolina to eastern Texas and the Mississippi Valley through the Ohio basin to southern Illinois; common in the coastal plains of the Carolinas

Food: aquatic insects, zooplankton

Reproduction: males guard small territories but do not build nests; eggs are laid in the vegetation and left with no parental care

Average Size: 1 to 1 1/2 inches

Records: none

Notes: Pygmy Sunfish are small, solitary fish that hide in dense vegetation and are most often seen when they enter minnow traps set near weedbeds. They look like tiny sunfish and were once thought to be a related species, though it has been deteremined they are unrelated and have been placed in their own family. There are four Pygmy Sunfish species found in the Carolinas. The Banded Sunfish is the most common and widespread; the Everglades Sunfish is a close second. Both species can be very abundant. Pygmy Sunfish adapt well to aquariums, and the Everglades Pygmy Sunfish has long been popular in the European pet trade.

99

Description: back is olive, blue-gray to black with worm-like markings; sides bronze to olive with red spots tinged light brown; lower fins red-orange with white leading edge; tail squared or slightly forked

Similar Species: Brown Trout (pg. 102), Rainbow Trout (pg. 104)

Brook Trout	**Brown Trout**	**Rainbow Trout**

worm-like marks, red spots	large dark spots, small red dots	pink stripe on silver body

BROOK TROUT

Salvelinus fontinalis

Salmonidae

Other Names: speckled, squaretail or coaster trout, brookie

Habitat: cool, clear streams and small lakes with moderate vegetation; prefers water temperatures of 50 to 60 degrees

Range: Great Lakes region north to Labrador, south through the Appalachians to Georgia, introduced widely; present in the mountains of North Carolina and the northern tip of South Carolina

Food: insects, small fish, leeches, crustaceans

Reproduction: spawns in late fall when water temperature reaches 40 to 49 degrees; female builds 4- to 12-inch-deep nest, then buries fertilized eggs in loose gravel; eggs hatch in 50 to 150 days

Average Size: 8 to 10 inches, 8 ounces

Records: NC—7 pounds, 7 ounces, Raven Fork River, 1980; SC—2 pounds, 6 ounces, Chattooga River, 1979; North American—14 pounds, 8 ounces, Nipigon River, Ontario, 1916

Notes: The Brook Trout is a beautiful fish native to the mountain streams of the Carolinas. Though there are still many wild populations of Brook Trout, they are not very tolerant of environmental change and many streams can no longer support them. Brook Trout are now routinely stocked in the Carolinas, but their numbers are sporadic due to poor water conditions, overfishing, or limited stocking. Their bright, orange flesh is firm and has a delicate flavor prized by trout fishermen.

101

BROWN TROUT

TIGER TROUT

Description: golden brown to olive back and sides; large dark spots on sides, the dorsal fin and sometimes the upper lobe of tail; red spots with light halos scattered along sides

Similar Species: Brook Trout (pg. 100), Rainbow Trout (pg. 104)

Brown Trout

dark spots on brown or olive background

Brook Trout

worm-like markings on back

Rainbow Trout

pink stripe on silvery body

BROWN TROUT
Salmo trutta

Other Names: German brown, Loch Leven or spotted trout

Habitat: open ocean near its spawning streams and clear, cold, gravel-bottomed streams; shallow portions of the Great Lakes

Range: Native to Europe from the Mediterranean to Siberia, introduced widely; present in the mountain streams of western North Carolina and northwestern South Carolina

Food: insects, crayfish, small fish

Reproduction: spawns in headwater streams, tributaries and stream mouths when migration is blocked; female fans out a saucer-shaped nest that male guards until spawning; female covers eggs

Average Size: 11 to 20 inches, 2 to 6 pounds

Records: NC—24 pounds, 10 ounces, Nantahala, 1998; SC—17 pounds, 9.5 ounces, Lake Jocassee, 1987; North American—40 pounds, 4 ounces, Little Red River, Arkansas, 1992

Notes: Brought to North America from Europe in the late 1800s, the Brown Trout was introduced here by the early 1900s. In many streams, Brown Trout replaced the native Brook Trout. Brown Trout prefer cold, clear streams, but will tolerate warmer water and turbidity better than other trout and also fare well in some lakes. Brown Trout are the favorite of fly fishermen around the world. They have a fine, delicate flavor. It is a secretive and hard-to-catch species, and often feeds at night. Many states have rules restricting night trout fishing. Brown Trout occasionally hybridize with Brook Trout to produce the colorful, but sterile, Tiger Trout. **103**

Description: blue-green to brown head and back; silver lower sides with pink to rose stripe; entire body covered with small black spots; adipose fin

Similar Species: Brook Trout (pg. 100), Brown Trout (pg. 102)

Rainbow Trout

pinkish stripe on silvery body

Brown Trout

sides lack pinkish stripe

Rainbow Trout

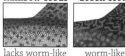

lacks worm-like markings

Brook Trout

worm-like marks on back

RAINBOW TROUT

Oncorhynchus mykiss

Salmonidae

Other Names: steelhead, Pacific, Kamloops or silver trout

Habitat: prefers whitewater in cool streams and coastal regions of large lakes; tolerates smaller, cool, clear lakes

Range: the Pacific Ocean and coastal streams from Mexico to Alaska, introduced worldwide; commonly stocked in mountain streams and lakes in western North Carolina and northwestern South Carolina

Food: insects, small crustaceans, fish

Reproduction: predominantly spring spawners but some fall-spawning varieties exist; female builds nest in well-aerated gravel in both streams and lakes

Average Size: 20 to 22 inches, 2 to 3 pounds

Records: NC—20 pounds, 3 ounces, Horsepasture River, Jackson County, 2006; SC—11 pounds, 5 ounces, Lake Jocassee, 1993; North American—42 pounds, 2 ounces, Bell Island, Alaska, 1970

Notes: This Pacific Trout was brought here over a hundred years ago, but attempts to establish a self-sustaining population were unsuccessful. This heavily fished species is maintained only through continuous restocking. Even so, it is the most common, widespread and popular trout in the Carolinas. Rainbow Trout are more tolerant of poor water conditions than other trout; some varieties can survive temperatures into the 80s. Steelhead Trout are Rainbow Trout that migrate from spawning streams into the open ocean or the Great Lakes as adults.   **105**

SPAWNING MALE

SPAWNING FEMALE

Description: greenish-blue back and bluntly pointed head; silver sides and belly; small black specks on the back and tail; 13 soft rays in anal fin; adipose fin; immature fish resemble trout; breeding males have bright green heads, red bodies and a well-developed kype (hooked snout)

Similar Species: Rainbow Trout (pg. 104)

Kokanee Salmon

Rainbow Trout

tiny black specks, none on back and tail

many black spots on back and tail

KOKANEE SALMON

Oncorhynchus nerka

Other Names: sockeye or red salmon, silver trout

Habitat: Kokanee—landlocked lakes, Sockeye—open ocean and large, clear, gravel-bottomed rivers

Range: Pacific Ocean north from California to Japan, coastal lakes in northeast North America, introduced in northeast U.S.; stocked in Nantahala reservoir in North Carolina

Food: plankton feeders

Reproduction: in the fall, 3-to-4-year-old Kokanee spawn in tributary streams or near lakeshore; females dig a redd (a shallow nest); adults die after spawning; young return to open water soon after hatching

Average Size: 8 to 12 inches, 1 to 2 pounds

Records: NC—3 pounds, 1 ounce, Nantahala Reservoir, 2007; SC—none; North American—9 pounds, 6 ounces, Okanagan Lake, British Columbia, 1988

Notes: The Kokanee Salmon is the landlocked form of the Sockeye Salmon and is stocked in the Nantahala Reservoir in North Carolina. Breeding adults resemble Rainbow Trout in shape but lack the pink stripe and black spots (some Kokanee may have tiny black specks on their sides but not on the back and tail). During spawning, the males are very distinctive with hooked beaks and bright colors. Though they primarily eat plankton, they can be caught with small spinner baits or flies and are very popular with some anglers. The flesh is oily and very good when smoked.

107

Description: slate gray to blotchy olive-brown back; large mouth; eyes set almost on top of head; large, wing-like pectoral fins; no scales

Similar Species: Tessellated Darter (pg. 80)

Mottled Sculpin	Tessellated Darter
distinctly scalloped anal fin	smooth, unscalloped anal fin

Mottled Sculpin	Tessellated Darter
lacks scales	scales present

MOTTLED SCULPIN

Cottus bairdii

Cottidae

Other Names: common sculpin, muddler, gudgeon

Habitat: bottom dwellers of cool, swift, hard-bottomed streams or wave-swept lakeshores with rocks or vegetation for cover

Range: eastern U.S. through Canada to Hudson Bay and the Rocky Mountains; mountainous regions of western North Carolina and northwestern South Carolina

Food: aquatic invertebrates, fish eggs, small fish

Reproduction: spawns in late spring when water temperature reaches 63 to 73 degrees; male builds a nest under ledges, logs or stream banks, then entices female with an elaborate courtship; female turns upside down to deposit eggs on the "roof" of the nest; male attends to nest through hatching

Average Size: 4 to 5 inches

Records: none

Notes: Sculpins are cold water fish, occupying mountain streams or deep, northern lakes. The Mottled Sculpin is the most common and widespread sculpin. This stream fish inhabits the same waters as Rainbow and Brown Trout, though it can tolerate somewhat warmer conditions than either trout. To a certain degree, Sculpins can modify their body color to blend in with the bottom. Mottled Sculpins are forage for many top predators and are a preferred bait when fishing for large Brown Trout.

Description: sides bright silver to silver-green with conspicuous light stripe; long, thin body; upturned mouth; 2 dorsal fins; tail deeply forked and pointed

Similar Species: Lined Topminnow, (pg. 170), Mosquitofish (pg. 62)

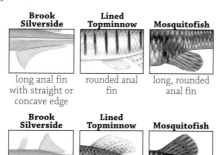

Brook Silverside	Lined Topminnow	Mosquitofish
long anal fin with straight or concave edge	rounded anal fin	long, rounded anal fin

Brook Silverside	Lined Topminnow	Mosquitofish
two dorsal fins	single dorsal fin	single dorsal fin

BROOK SILVERSIDE

Labidesthes sicculus

Atherinidae

Other Names: northern silverside, skipjack, friar

Habitat: surface of clear lakes; slack water of large streams

Range: Great Lake states south through the central U.S. to the Gulf States; common in southern South Carolina

Food: aquatic and flying insects

Reproduction: spawns in late spring and early summer; eggs are laid in sticky strings attached to vegetation; most adults die after spawning

Average Size: 3 to 4 inches

Records: none

Notes: The Brook Silverside is a member of a large family of primarily marine fish that live mostly in tropical and sub-tropical regions. It is a flashy fish that is often seen cruising near the surface in small schools. Its upturned mouth is an adaptation to surface feeding. It is not uncommon to see a Brook Silverside make spectacular leaps from the water, flying fish style, in pursuit of prey. The Silverside has a short lifespan, often lasting only 15 months.

Description: dark brown back fading to lighter brown sides with irregular blotches; large scales on head; large mouth with sharp teeth; long, single dorsal fin

Similar Species: Bowfin (pg. 24)

Northern Snakehead

enlarged scales on head

Bowfin

no head scales, bony plates between jaws

Northern Snakehead

pelvic fins near head, long anal fin

Bowfin

pelvic fins at mid body, short anal fin

NORTHERN SNAKEHEAD

Channa argus

Other Names: amur or ocellated snakehead, "frankenfish"

Habitat: stagnant, shallow ponds and slow-moving streams with a muddy or weedy bottom

Range: native to China and Korea. introduced to Japan, Eastern Europe and five U.S. states; Wylie Lake and Catawba River in North Carolina

Food: fish, crayfish, frogs

Reproduction: females can spawn several times a year beginning in June and lay 100,000 eggs

Average Size: 12 to 24 inches, 2 to 5 pounds

Records: none

Notes: Northern Snakeheads were brought to the U.S. for live fish markets and as aquarium pets, then they escaped or were released. Several Snakeheads have been found in Wylie Lake and the Catawba River, but the species is not thought to be established. They have a modified swim bladder that allows them to breathe air and they can slither through wet marshes for up to three days to reach new lakes. Snakeheads are voracious predators that can tolerate temperatures from freezing to near 90 degrees. This highly competitive invader has the potential to devastate native fish populations. Anglers should learn to identify Snakeheads; if any Snakeheads are caught, they should be killed, frozen and given to a conservation officer.

Description: color variable, side with eyes, mottled light to dark brown or olive green with 6 to 8 dark bands across the body; mottled fins; side without eyes, white; flat flounder-like body with eyes on top; tiny rough scales giving body a hairy texture

Similar Species: Southern Flounder (pg. 60)

Hogchoker

dorsal fin
extends to
mouth

Summmer Flounder

dorsal and anal
fins extend to
head

HOGCHOKER
Trinectes maculatus

Other Names: Hogchoker flounder

Habitat: marine areas; freshwater streams with open sand or silt bottom

Range: Atlantic coast from Massachusetts to Venezuela, Gulf coast from Florida to Texas; common in the coastal rivers of the Carolinas

Food: crustaceans and aquatic insects

Reproduction: in early summer, adults return to marine estuaries to spawn; after hatching, larvae migrates up freshwater streams to mature; a 6-inch female may contain over 50,000 eggs

Average Size: 4 to 6 inches

Records: none

Notes: Hogchokers are plentiful, coastal river fish that are most often encountered when caught in crab traps, fish traps or nets. Once caught, Hogchokers quickly attach themselves to nets, buckets and fishermen. For this reason, Hogchokers leave a lasting impression. The spiny scales and feathery fins give Hogchokers a fuzzy feeling when handled. Hogchokers were reportedly named because the fish lodged in pigs' throats after hogs were fed the commonly netted fish.

ATLANTIC STURGEON

SHORTNOSE STURGEON

Description: Atlantic—slate gray back and sides; snout long with a narrow mouth; two rows of scutes (bony plates) before anus; Shortnose—dark brown to black back and sides; snout short with large, wide mouth; both—five rows of scutes (bony plates), one on back, two on sides, two on bottom; tail shark-like with the upper lobe much longer than lower

Similar Species: Atlantic Sturgeon (pg. 116), Shortnose Sturgeon (pg. 116)

Atlantic Sturgeon	Shortnose Sturgeon
long snout, white on leading edge of paired fins	short snout, white on trailing edge of paired fins

116

ATLANTIC STURGEON

Acipenser oxyrhynchu

SHORTNOSE STURGEON *Acipenser brevirostrum*

Other Names: none

Habitat: large coastal rivers and estuaries

Range: Atlantic—Atlantic coast from Labrador to Florida, the Gulf Coast to the Mississippi River; possible in any coastal streams of the Carolinas; Shortnose—Atlantic coast from New Brunswick to Central Florida; coastal streams of NC and southern SC

Food: snails, clams, crayfish and insects

Reproduction: migrates to brackish estuaries or freshwater rivers to spawn; thousands of eggs are laid and fertilized a few at a time in the current of large rivers

Average Size: Atlantic—8 to 12 feet, 300 to 400 pounds; Shortnose—2 to 3 feet, 6 to 8 pounds

Records: none

Notes: Once an important commercial fish harvested for both meat and caviar, both species are either threatened or endangered. One is most likely to find Shortnose Sturgeon in South Carolina. The Atlantic Sturgeon is not as rare and is still occasionally caught offshore and in larger rivers. Because of its shark-like tail, the sturgeon is often mistaken for a shark in coastal regions. The small, toothless mouth makes them easy to identify. Any sightings should be reported to the Fish and Game Department, and every attempt should be made to return a hooked fish to the water.

117

Description: slate-green back with bronze sides; large dark eye; deep, laterally compressed body; rounded head; blunt snout; small downturned mouth with thick lips

Similar Species: Common Carp (pg. 66)

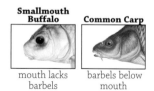

Smallmouth Buffalo
mouth lacks barbels

Common Carp
barbels below mouth

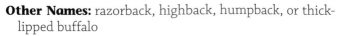

SMALLMOUTH BUFFALO

Ictiobus bubalus

Other Names: razorback, highback, humpback, or thick-lipped buffalo

Habitat: moderate to swift currents in the deep, clean waters of larger streams and some lakes

Range: the Missouri, Mississippi and Ohio River drainages south to the Gulf and west into New Mexico; common in larger rivers of western North Carolina and central North and South Carolina

Food: small mollusks, aquatic insect larvae and zooplankton

Reproduction: spawns in clear, shallow water of fields and marshes when water temperature reaches the low 60s; young quickly return to main streams when water recedes

Average Size: 18 to 20 inches, 10 to 12 pounds

Records: NC—88 pounds, Lake Wylie, 1993 (not registered as a N.A. record); SC—none; North American—73 pounds, 1 ounce, Lake Koshkonong, Wisconsin, 2004

Notes: There are three sucker species in North America; the Smallmouth Buffalo is the only species routinely found in the Carolinas. It requires deep, clean water and feeds heavily on aquatic insect larvae. The Smallmouth Buffalo is commercially harvested in the Pee Dee River and is highly respected as table fare. The Smallmouth Buffalo is a powerful fighter and can be a challenge to land when hooked near fast current. Few Buffalo are taken by anglers, but they can be caught by using small insect baits floated near the bottom.

Description: bright silver back and sides, often with a yellow
tinge; fins clear; deep body with round, blunt head; leading
edge of dorsal fin extends into a large, arching "quill"

Similar Species: Common Carp (pg. 66)

Quillback **Common Carp**

mouth lacks   barbels below
barbels   mouth

QUILLBACK

Carpiodes cyprinus

Catostomidae

Other Names: silver carp, carpsucker, lake quillback

Habitat: slow-flowing streams and rivers; backwaters and lakes, particularly areas with soft bottoms

Range: south-central Canada through the Great Lakes to the eastern U.S.; south through the Mississippi drainage to the Gulf; common in most of the upper reaches of the major rivers in the Carolinas

Food: insects, plant matter, decaying bottom material

Reproduction: spawns in late spring through early summer in tributaries or lake shallows; eggs are deposited in open areas over sand or a mud bottom

Average Size: 12 to 14 inches, 1 to 3 pounds

Records: NC—none; SC—none; North American—8 pounds, 13 ounces, Lake Winnebago, Wisconsin, 2003

Notes: In North America, there are four fish known as carp-suckers; three are found in the Carolinas. The Quillback is the most common and widespread species. Quillbacks prefer medium to large rivers and lakes, and even though they are relatively rare in the Carolinas, they can be a locally common fish. They are a schooling fish that filter feed along the bottom. Not often sought by anglers, they readily take wet flies and can be strong fighters when caught on light tackle. The flesh is white and very flavorful.

Description: dark gray-brown back; yellow to brassy sides; off-white belly; dull red to orange fins and tail; blunt nose; downturned sucker mouth

Similar Species: Creek Chubsucker (pg. 124), Hog Sucker (pg. 126), White Sucker (pg. 128)

Shorthead Redhorse	**Creek Chubsucker**	**White Sucker**
deeply forked, pointed tail	slightly forked, rounded tail	slightly forked, rounded tail

Shorthead Redhorse	**Northern Hog Sucker**
head flat to raised between eyes	head concave between eyes

SHORTHEAD REDHORSE

Moxostoma macrolepidotum

Other Names: none

Habitat: clean streams and rivers with hard bottoms; clear lakes with strong-flowing tributary streams

Range: Central Canada and the U.S. through the Atlantic States; common in central North and South Carolina

Food: aquatic insects, small crustaceans, plant debris

Reproduction: spawns from late May to June when the water reaches the low 60s; adults migrate into small tributary streams to lay eggs on shallow gravel bars in swift current near deep pools

Average Size: 18 to 24 inches, 2 to 5 pounds

Records: NC—none; SC—none; North American-—11 pounds, 5 ounces, Brunet River, Wisconsin, 1983

Notes: There are a half dozen Redhorse species in the Carolinas, and they range from two to ten pounds in size. All Redhorses are "sucker type fish," and are similar in appearance and hard to tell apart. They may look alike, but each is a separate species and occupies its own niche. They are cleanwater fish and are very susceptible to increased turbidity and pollutants. Redhorses are primarily stream fish; the Shorthead Redhorse is the exception, inhabiting lakes as well as streams. It is also one of the largest, most common and widespread species but is not often targeted by anglers. Even so, it is caught fairly often by river anglers, fights well on light tackle, and readily takes larger wet flies. The flesh is bony but has a good flavor when smoked. **123**

Description: olive brown back; yellow to olive sides with a dark band that may appear as connected blotches; creamy yellow belly; scales have distinct dark edges

Similar Species: Hog Sucker (pg. 126), Shorthead Redhorse (pg. 122), White Sucker (pg. 128)

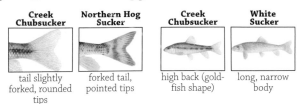

Creek Chubsucker	Northern Hog Sucker	Creek Chubsucker	White Sucker
tail slightly forked, rounded tips	forked tail, pointed tips	high back (gold-fish shape)	long, narrow body

CREEK CHUBSUCKER

Erimyzon oblongus

Other Names: sweet or yellow sucker

Habitat: sluggish pools of small to medium-sized streams and clear lakes

Range: the Atlantic coast from north Georgia to Maine, the Mississippi River drainage north to the southern Great Lakes; common in the Piedmont and coastal plains of the Carolinas

Food: small crustaceans, aquatic insects

Reproduction: spawning takes place in April and May when water reaches the 60s; a shallow nest is excavated in sand or gravel of small tributary streams; males aggressively defend breeding territories around nest; eggs and young are not guarded

Average Size: 8 to 14 inches

Records: none

Notes: The Creek Chubsucker is one of the most important forage fish in many small Carolina lakes and streams. Chubsuckers are very prolific and even a small number of breeding adults in a lake can produce large numbers of fry for game fish to feed on. They fare well on a hook and in the bait pail, making them ideal large bait minnows. Chubsuckers readily take a worm-baited hook and can pro-vide great sport for young kids spending a day on the creek.

Description: back is dark olive brown fading to yellow-brown blotches on the sides; 4 to 5 irregular dark saddles; elongated body almost round in cross section; large head that is concave between the eyes; lower fins are dull red

Similar Species: Shorthead Redhorse (pg. 122), White Sucker (pg. 128)

Northern Hog Sucker	Shorthead Redhorse	White Sucker
head concave between eyes	head flat to raised between eyes	head flat to raised between eyes

NORTHERN HOG SUCKER

Hypentelium nigricans

Other Names: hog molly, hammerhead, riffle or bigheaded sucker, crawl-a-bottom

Habitat: riffles and tailwaters of clear streams with hard bottoms; found in a few lakes near the mouths of tributary streams

Range: central and eastern Canada and the U.S. south to Alabama and west to Oklahoma; common in the mountains of both North and South Carolina and the Piedmont of north-central NC

Food: small crustaceans, aquatic insects

Reproduction: spawns in April and May when water reaches the low 60s; males gather in riffles or downstream pools; females enter spawning areas just long enough to drop eggs, which are quickly fertilized by several males; no parental care

Average Size: 10 to 12 inches, 1 pound

Records: NC—none; SC— none; North American—1 pound, 12 ounces, Fox River, Wisconsin, 2004

Notes: Northern Hog Suckers are clean water fish and well adapted to feed in moving water. They use their elongated shape and concave head to hold their place in riffles while turning over stones to release food. It is common for other fish to follow Hog Suckers to feed on what is stirred up. Hog Suckers are not of much interest to anglers but are sometimes caught by trout fishermen working the edge of fast water. **127**

Description: olive to brownish back; sides gray to silver; belly off-white; dorsal and tail fin slate; the lower fins tinged orange; snout barely extends beyond upper lip

Similar Species: Creek Chubsucker (pg. 124), Hog Sucker (pg. 126), Shorthead Redhorse (pg. 122)

White Sucker

long, narrow body

Creek Chubsucker

high back (gold-fish shape)

White Sucker

head flat to raised between eyes

Northern Hog Sucker

concave head between eyes

White Sucker

slightly forked, rounded tail

Shorthead Redhorse

deeply forked, pointed tail

WHITE SUCKER
Catostomus commersonii

Catostomidae

Other Names: common, coarse-scaled or eastern sucker, black mullet, bay fish

Habitat: clear to turbid (cloudy) streams, rivers and lakes

Range: Canada through the central and eastern U.S. south from New Mexico to South Carolina; common in the upper Piedmont and mountain regions of the Carolinas

Food: insects, crustaceans, plant matter

Reproduction: spawns in early spring when water reaches the high 50s to low 60s; adults spawn in tributary riffles over gravel or coarse sand; in lakes, eggs are deposited over shallow gravel or rocks along wave swept shorelines

Average Size: 12 to 18 inches, 1 to 3 pounds

Records: NC—none; SC—none; North American—7 pounds, 4 ounces, Big Round Lake, Wisconsin, 1978

Notes: The White Sucker is one of the most common fish in the rivers and lakes of the central and western Carolinas and one of the most important. Highly productive, it provides a large source of forage for game fish and is a mainstay in the bait industry in many areas. White Suckers are not the great consumers of trout eggs they were once thought to be, but may compete with trout fry for food when first hatched. The tremendous forage source young White Suckers provide for game fish offsets this competition. White Suckers are most often fished during the spring spawning run. The flesh is firm with a fine flavor and is oily enough to make excellent smoked fish.

129

Description: dark green back; greenish sides often with dark lateral band; belly white to gray; large forward-facing mouth; lower jaw extends to rear margin of eye

Similar Species: Smallmouth Bass (pg. 134), Spotted Bass (pg. 136)

Largemouth Bass	Smallmouth Bass	Spotted Bass
mouth extends well beyond non-red eye	mouth does not extend beyond red eye	jaw does not extend much beyond eye

LARGEMOUTH BASS

Micropterus salmoides

Centrarchidae

Other Names: black, bayou, green or slough bass, green trout

Habitat: shallow, fertile, weedy lakes and river backwaters; weedy bays and extensive weedbeds of large lakes

Range: southern Canada through the United States into Mexico, extensively introduced throughout the world; common throughout the Carolinas

Food: small fish, frogs, insects, crayfish

Reproduction: spawns when water temperature reaches 60 degrees; male builds nest in small clearings in weedbeds 2 to 8 feet deep; male guards nest and fry until the "brood swarm" disperses

Average Size: 12 to 20 inches, 1 to 5 pounds

Records: NC—15 pounds, 14 ounces, farm pond, Union County, 1991; SC—16 pounds, 2 ounces, Lake Marion, 1949; North American—22 pounds, 4 ounces, Montgomery Lake, Georgia, 1932

Notes: The Largemouth Bass is the most sought after game fish in North America. These denizens of the weedbeds are voracious carnivores and will eat anything that fits into their mouth. Largemouths are common in lakes and wide streams with weedbeds less than 20 feet deep. Largemouths are often one to three pounds, but eight and nine pound fish are not uncommon. They are fine table fare when under two pounds and taken from clear water, but are not known for table quality when large or taken from muddy water.

Description: green to black back; green-brown sides with dark bars; dark spot on gill; red eye; dark stripes; lower jaw extends to the eye; shallow notch between dorsal fins; scales on the base of dorsal and anal fins

Similar Species: Smallmouth Bass (pg. 134), Spotted Bass (pg. 136)

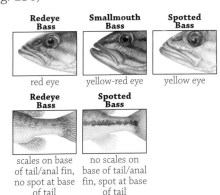

Redeye Bass — red eye

Smallmouth Bass — yellow-red eye

Spotted Bass — yellow eye

Redeye Bass — scales on base of tail/anal fin, no spot at base of tail

Spotted Bass — no scales on base of tail/anal fin, spot at base of tail

REDEYE BASS

Micropterus coosae

Other Names: Flint River bass

Habitat: rocky shallows in rivers and small streams

Range: Alabama, Georgia and the Carolinas; southwestern SC and western NC, native to the upper Savannah River drainage, stocked in Lake Hartwell

Food: small fish, frogs, insects and crayfish

Reproduction: migrates up small tributary streams to spawn when water temperature reaches 60 degrees; males build nest then guard the nest and fry; does not reproduce well in waters without a current

Average Size: 10 to 12 inches, 12 ounces to 1 pound

Records: NC—none; SC—5 pounds, 2 ounces, Lake Jocassee, 2001; North American—8 pounds, 3 ounces, Flint River, Georgia, 1977

Notes: The Redeye Bass is a small bass, averaging under a pound in size, with a very restricted range. Redeyes are similar in appearance and habits to Smallmouth Bass but can be quickly distinguished by the red eyes and fins. Redeye Bass may be found in a few lakes or reservoirs but prefer small tributary streams and can only reproduce where there is a current. Due to their small size and rarity, they are not popular among bass fishermen but they have a small, but loyal, following with some fly fishermen.

Description: back and sides mottled dark green to bronze or pale gold, often with dark vertical bands; white belly; stout body; large, forward-facing mouth; red eye

Similar Species: Largemouth Bass (pg. 130), Redeye Bass (pg. 132), Spotted Bass (pg. 136)

Smallmouth Bass	Largemouth Bass	Redeye Bass	Spotted Bass
yellow/red eye, small mouth	yellow eye, large mouth	red eye, small mouth	yellow eye, small mouth

Smallmouth Bass	Spotted Bass
scales on base of tail/anal fins, no spot at base of tail	no scales on base of tail/anal fin, spot at base of tail

SMALLMOUTH BASS

Micropterus dolomieu

Centrarchidae

Other Names: bronzeback, brown or redeye bass, redeye

Habitat: clear, swift-flowing streams and rivers; clear lakes with gravel or rocky shorelines

Range: extensively introduced throughout North America, Europe and Asia, common in the Great Lakes; present in the mountainous regions of the Carolinas

Food: insects, small fish, crayfish

Reproduction: male builds a nest in 3 to 10 feet of water over open gravel beds when water temperatures reach the mid-to-high 60s; nest is often near logs or boulders; male aggressively guards the nest and young until fry disperse

Average Size: 12 to 20 inches, 1 to 4 pounds

Records: NC—10 pounds, 2 ounces, Hiwassee Reservoir, 1991; SC—9 pounds, 7 ounces, Lake Jocassee, 2001; North American—11 pounds, 15 ounces, Dale Hollow Lake, Tennessee, 1955

Notes: Smallmouth Bass are a world-class game fish noted for strong fights and acrobatic jumps. Native to the cooler portions of the Carolinas, they have been extensively introduced throughout the world. Though the range of this slowly-maturing fish has expanded, its numbers are deceasing due to overfishing and habitat loss. Smallmouth Bass prefer deeper water than the weedbeds preferred by its larger cousin, the Largemouth Bass. The flesh is firm, succulent, and regarded by some anglers as second only to Walleye as table fare.

135

Description: dark green back with light green sides; side blotches form a dark stripe, with dark spots above; light spots on each scale below; dark lines extend from red eye

Similar Species: Redeye Bass (pg. 132), Smallmouth Bass (pg. 134), Spotted Bass (pg. 136)

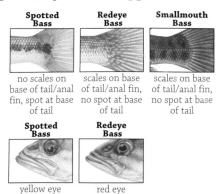

Spotted Bass	Redeye Bass	Smallmouth Bass
no scales on base of tail/anal fin, spot at base of tail	scales on base of tail/anal fin, no spot at base of tail	scales on base of tail/anal fin, no spot at base of tail

Spotted Bass	Redeye Bass
yellow eye	red eye

SPOTTED BASS

Centrarchidae

Micropterus punctulatus

Other Names: Kentucky, speckled or yellow bass, spottys

Habitat: deep, silted pools in sluggish, medium to large streams; larger lakes and reservoirs

Range: the Ohio and Mississippi drainage in the southern U.S. from Florida to Texas; native to western North Carolina and introduced to the Cape Fear River Drainage

Food: small fish and crayfish

Reproduction: when water temperatures reach the mid-to-high 60s in May and June, males build a nest in open gravel beds 3 to 4 feet deep; male aggressively guards the nest and young

Average Size: 8 to 18 inches, 8 ounces to 2 pounds

Records: NC—6 pounds, 5 ounces, Lake Norman, 2003; SC—8 pounds, 2 ounces, Lake Jocassee, 2001; North American—10 pounds, 4 ounces, Pine Flat Lake, California, 2001

Notes: The Spotted Bass has a rather restricted range in North Carolina but is very abundant within that range. In terms of habit, Spotted Bass share traits with both Largemouth and Smallmouth Bass. Spotted Bass are found in slower, deep pools, whereas Smallmouths prefer stream riffles and Largemouths inhabit the edges of weedbeds. In reservoirs, Spotted Bass seek deeper water than Smallmouth Bass. Spotted Bass can tolerate higher turbidity than other bass, but in most areas, they are somewhat smaller than either Largemouths or Smallmouths.

137

Description: black to olive back; silver sides with dark green to black blotches; back more arched and depression above eye more pronounced than White Crappie

Similar Species: White Crappie (pg. 140)

Black Crappie	White Crappie	Black Crappie	White Crappie
usually 7 to 8 spines in dorsal fin	usually 5 to 6 spines in dorsal fin	dorsal fin length equal to distance from dorsal to eye	dorsal fin shorter than distance from eye to dorsal

BLACK CRAPPIE

Pomoxis nigromaculatus

Other Names: speckled perch, speck, papermouth

Habitat: quiet, clear water of streams and midsized lakes; often associated with vegetation but may roam over deep, open basins and flats, particularly during winter

Range: southern Manitoba through the Atlantic and south-eastern states, introduced in the West; common throughout the Carolinas

Food: small fish, aquatic insects, zooplankton

Reproduction: spawns in shallow weedbeds from May to June when water temperatures reach the high 50s; male builds circular nest in fine gravel or sand and then guards the eggs and young until fry begin feeding

Average Size: 7 to 12 inches, 8 ounces to 1 pound

Records: NC—4 pounds, 15 ounces, Asheboro City Lake #4, 1980; SC—5 pounds, Lake Moultrie, 1957; North American—6 pounds, Westwego Canal, Louisiana, 1969

Notes: The Black Crappie is the most widespread Crappie species in North America and native to the Atlantic seaboard. They are found in most lakes and slow-moving streams in the Carolinas with clear water and good vegetative growth. Black Crappies are a schooling fish, and when not spawning, are often found suspended in deeper water. They nest in colonies and frequently gather in large feeding schools in winter. Black Crappies are sought for their sweet-tasting, white fillets but not for their fighting ability.

139

Description: greenish back; silvery green to white sides with 7 to 9 dark vertical bars; the only sunfish with six spines in both the dorsal and anal fin

Similar Species: Black Crappie (pg. 138)

White Crappie	**Black Crappie**	**White Crappie**	**Black Crappie**
usually 5 to 6 spines in dorsal fin	usually 7 to 8 spines in dorsal fin	dorsal fin shorter than distance from eye to dorsal	dorsal fin length equal to distance from dorsal to eye

WHITE CRAPPIE

Pomoxis annularis

Centrarchidae

Other Names: silver, pale or ringed crappie, papermouth

Habitat: slightly silty streams and midsized lakes; prefers less vegetation than Black Crappie

Range: North Dakota south and east to the Gulf and Atlantic states except peninsular Florida; common throughout the Carolinas

Food: aquatic insects, zooplankton, small fish

Reproduction: spawns on a firm sand or gravel bottom when water temperatures approach 60 degrees; male builds shallow, round nest; male guards eggs and young after spawning

Average Size: 8 to 10 inches, 5 to 16 ounces

Records: NC—1 pound, 13 ounces, Lake Norman, 2007; SC—5 pounds, 1 ounce, Lake Murray, 1949; North America—5 pounds, 3 ounces, Enid Dam, Mississippi, 1957

Notes: Native to the Mississippi River drainage, they have been widely introduced and are now widespread but are not as common as Black Crappies in the Carolinas. They prefer deeper, less vegetated and more turbid (cloudy) water than Black Crappies. Due to its tolerance of turbid water, there is some indication of a positive relation between the Common Carp and the White Crappie. Both Black and White Crappies actively feed during the winter, ensuring that they are the most popular panfish during the ice fishing season.

141

Description: olive green to silver-green back and sides; longitudinal stripes of brown spots on sides; dark wedge-shaped bar under eye; latterly compressed body; anal and dorsal fin nearly equal length; dark spot on dorsal fin of young fish; small mouth

Similar Species: Black Crappie (pg. 138)

Flier	**Black Crappie**	**Flier**	**Black Crappie**
10 to 13 dorsal spines	6 to 8 dorsal spines	small mouth, dark bar under eye	large mouth, no dark bar under eye

FLIER

Centrarchus macropterus

Centrarchidae

Other Names: spotfin, silver, round or swamp sunfish

Habitat: weedy, quiet, waters with a soft bottom in lakes, creeks and coastal swamps

Range: coastal states from Virginia to eastern Texas, Mississippi Valley through the Ohio Valley; common in the coastal plains of the Carolinas

Food: aquatic insects, zooplankton, small fish

Reproduction: nests in late spring or early summer in dense vegetation; nests are solitary or in small groups; males guard nest and young

Average Size: 4 to 6 inches, four ounces

Records: NC—1 pound, 5 ounces, private pond, 1990, (not recorded as a NA record); SC—1 pound, 4 ounces, Hemingway, 1977, (not recorded as a NA record); North American—1 pound, 2 ounces, Pope's Pond, Georgia, 1995

Notes: Fliers are small sunfish native to the southern Atlantic coast. This sunfish can withstand low oxygen levels and higher acidity than most other sunfish. It is very common in still, swampy water. Rarely over 6 inches long, Fliers are too small to be an important panfish but they readily bite and can be proficient bait robbers. When large enough to eat, Fliers have flaky, white flesh and fine flavor. Though not a prized panfish, fliers are good predators on mosquito larvae, and small ones should be carefully returned to the water.

Description: dark olive to green on back, blending to silver-gray, copper, orange, purple or brown on sides; 5 to 9 dark vertical bars on sides that fade with age; yellow belly and copper breast; large, dark gill spot; dark spot on dorsal fin

Similar Species: Green Sunfish (pg. 148), Pumpkinseed (pg. 150), Redbreast Sunfish (pg. 152)

Bluegill	**Green Sunfish**	**Bluegill**	**Redbreast Sunfish**
small mouth	large mouth	long, pointed pectoral fin	short round pectoral fin

Bluegill	**Pumpkinseed**	**Redbreast Sunfish**
dark gill spot on rounded gill flap	red-orange margin on gill spot	long, narrow gill flap

BLUEGILL

Lepomis macrochirus

Centrarchidae

Other Names: bream, sun perch, blue sunfish, copperbelly, strawberry bass

Habitat: medium to large streams and most lakes with weedy bays or shorelines

Range: southern Canada through the southern states into Mexico; common throughout the Carolinas

Food: aquatic insects, snails, small fish

Reproduction: spawns from when water temperature reaches the high 60s to low 80s; male builds a nest in vegetation in a colony of other nests; male guards nest and fry

Average Size: 6 to 9 inches, 5 to 8 ounces

Records: NC—4 pounds, 5 ounces, Henderson County, 1967; SC—3 pounds, 4 ounces, Lancaster County, 1973; North American—4 pounds, 12 ounces, Ketona Lake, Alabama, 1950

Notes: Bluegills are native to the Carolinas and are the most popular panfish here and throughout the United States. They have small mouths and feed mostly on aquatic insects and small fish. Bluegills feed on the surface more frequently than other panfish, making them popular with fly fishermen, though some bluegills prefer deep weedbeds at the edge of open water. Many lakes have large populations of hybrid sunfish, crosses between Bluegills and Green or Pumpkinseed Sunfish. Painted Bream are not a separate species, but a strain of bluegills with a pink throat and dark blotches on the sides.

145

Description: dark olive to black back and sides fading to light olive belly; blue-green spots run in lines down sides; small dark gill spot; tail rounded

Similar Species: Pumpkinseed (pg. 150), Redbreast Sunfish (pg. 152)

Bluespotted Sunfish	**Pumpkinseed**	**Redbreast Sunfish**
small, dark gill spot	red/orange margin on gill spot	long, narrow gill flap

Bluespotted Sunfish	**Pumpkinseed**	**Redbreast Sunfish**
short, round pectoral fin	long, pointed pectoral fin	short, round pectoral fin

BLUESPOTTED SUNFISH

Centrarchidae

Enneacanthus gloriosus

Other Names: spotted or bluedot sunfish

Habitat: shallow, weedy lakes and river backwaters

Range: the Atlantic drainage from southern New York to Florida; common in the coastal plains of the Carolinas

Food: aquatic insects, crustaceans

Reproduction: spawns in May and June when water temperatures reach the high 60s; male builds a small, round nest in weedbeds and defends the nest and young

Average Size: 3 to 4 inches

Records: none

Notes: There are three species in the genus *Enneacanthus* found in the Carolinas: the Banded Sunfish, the Blackbanded Sunfish and the Bluespotted Sunfish. All are similar in appearance and habits. The Bluespotted Sunfish is the most common species and can be very abundant in the waters of the coastal plains. Bluespotted Sunfish are not large enough to be of any value to anglers but are prolific and an important forage fish for larger game fish. They can occupy water with an oxygen content lower than other sunfish and may be very important in mosquito control in some areas. The breeding males are brightly colored and make great aquarium fish.

Description: dark green back with dark olive to bluish sides; yellow to cream belly; scales flecked with yellow, producing a brassy appearance; dark gill spot with a light margin; large mouth and thick lips

Similar Species: Bluegill (pg. 144), Redear Sunfish (pg. 154)

Green Sunfish	Bluegill	Redear Sunfish
prominent light margin on rounded gill spot	round gill spot with clear margin	red-orange margin on gill spot

Green Sunfish	Redear Sunfish

blue stripes on head	no blue stripes on head

GREEN SUNFISH

Centrarchidae

Lepomis cyanellus

Other Names: green perch, sand bass

Habitat: warm, weedy, shallow lakes and the backwaters of slow-moving streams

Range: most of the United States into Mexico excluding Florida and the Rocky Mountains; native to western North Carolina, introduced to the central Piedmont region

Food: aquatic insects, small crustaceans, fish

Reproduction: male builds nest in less than a foot of weedy water in temperatures from 60 to 80 degrees; may produce two broods per year; male guards nest and fans eggs until hatching

Average Size: 4 to 6 inches, less than 8 ounces

Records: NC—1 pound, 2 ounces, Butner-Falls Neuse Game Land, 2006; SC—none; North American—2 pounds, 2 ounces, Stockton Lake, Missouri, 1971

Notes: Green Sunfish are often mistaken for Bluegills but are not as deep-bodied and prefer shallower weedbeds. Very tolerant of turbid water and low oxygen levels, they thrive in warm, weedy lakes and backwaters. Green Sunfish stunt easily, filling some lakes with three-inch-long "potato chips." Green Sunfish sometimes hybridize with other sunfish species, producing large, aggressive offspring, but these crosses result in poor panfish populations overall.

149

Description: back brown to olive fading to light olive; orange-yellow spots on sides, with 7 to 10 vertical bands; black gill spot with light margin and orange or red crescent

Similar Species: Bluegill (pg. 144), Green Sunfish (pg. 148), Redbreast Sunfish (pg. 152)

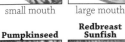

Pumpkinseed
small mouth

Green Sunfish
large mouth

Pumpkinseed
long, pointed pectoral fin

Redbreast Sunfish
short, round pectoral fin

Pumpkinseed
red-orange margin on gill spot

Redbreast Sunfish
gill flap lacks orange or red margin

PUMPKINSEED

Lepomis gibbosus

Centrarchidae

Other Names: yellow or round sunfish, sun bass, bream

Habitat: weedy ponds, clear lakes, reservoirs and slow moving streams; prefers slightly cooler water than Bluegills

Range: central and eastern North America, introduced in the West; common in most of the Carolinas except western NC and the Savannah River area of SC

Food: snails, aquatic and terrestrial insects, small fish

Reproduction: spawns when water temperatures reach 55 to 63 degrees; male builds a nest among weeds in less than two feet of water over a sand or gravel bottom; male aggressively guards the nest; may produce multiple broods

Average Size: 6 to 8 inches, 5 to 8 ounces

Records: NC—1 pound, 6 ounces, Trent River, 2003; SC—2 pounds, 4 ounces, North Saluda River, 1997; North American—2 pounds, 4 ounces, North Saluda River, South Carolina, 1997

Notes: This small, brightly colored sunfish is one of the most well-known and beautiful fish native to Carolinas. Pumpkinseeds often gather in small schools around docks and submerged deadfalls. They prefer slightly cooler and more open water than Bluegills. They readily hybridize with other sunfish, and the hybrids may totally colonize some lakes. Pumpkinseeds commonly stunt, filling lakes with two-and-a-half-inch breeding adults. Pumpkinseeds aggressively attack small natural and artificial bait, and large specimens provide fine table fare. **151**

Description: dark olive green back; olive sides; gray-white belly; bright yellow-orange breast; gill flap long, black and narrower than the eye; tail slightly forked

Similar Species: Bluegill (pg. 144), Bluespotted Sunfish (pg. 146), Pumpkinseed (pg. 150)

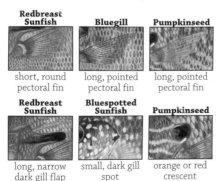

Redbreast Sunfish	Bluegill	Pumpkinseed
short, round pectoral fin	long, pointed pectoral fin	long, pointed pectoral fin

Redbreast Sunfish	Bluespotted Sunfish	Pumpkinseed
long, narrow dark gill flap	small, dark gill spot	orange or red crescent

REDBREAST SUNFISH

Centrarchidae

Lepomis auritus

Other Names: yellowbelly or longear sunfish, sun perch, redbreast bream

Habitat: rocky riffles in streams with medium current; occasionally lakes or reservoirs

Range: Atlantic drainage from southern New York to Florida; common throughout the Carolinas

Food: aquatic insects, crustaceans, small fish

Reproduction: spawns in May and June when water temperature reaches the high 60s; male builds a small, round nest in weedbeds away from the current; male defends nest

Average Size: 4 to 8 inches, 4 ounces

Records: NC—1 pound, 12 ounces, Bladen County Big Swamp, 1983; SC—2 pounds, Lumber River, 1975; North American—2 pounds, 1 ounce, Suwannee River, Florida, 1988

Notes: The Redbreast Sunfish is a small sunfish native to the Atlantic drainage east of the Alleghenies and has been introduced throughout the Southeast. It prefer streams, but is frequently found in reservoirs and impoundments. Redbreast Sunfish are often found around rocks, logs or undercut banks near moving water and are slightly more nocturnal than other sunfish. A popular panfish in some areas, they bite aggressively on small artificial lures and live bait both day and night.

Description: back and sides bronze to dark green, fading to light green; sides have faint vertical bars and small spots; bluish stripes on side of head; gill flap short with dark spot and red margin in males; breast yellow or orange

Similar Species: Bluegill (pg. 144), Redbreast Sunfish (pg. 152)

Redear Sunfish

red-orange margin on gill spot

Bluegill

round gill spot with clear margin

Redbreast Sunfish

long, narrow, dark gill flap

REDEAR SUNFISH

Lepomis microlophus

Centrarchidae

Other Names: shellcracker, stumpknocker, yellow bream

Habitat: congregates around stumps and logs in low to moderate vegetation in lakes and swamps and large, quiet streams; prefers sand or gravel bottoms, frequents brackish water

Range: the northern Midwest through the South, introduced in the West; common throughout the Carolinas except in the mountainous regions

Food: mainly mollusks

Reproduction: males build and guard nest in shallow, vegetated water in spring when water temperatures reach high 60s; may produce second brood well into summer

Average Size: 8 to 10 inches, 8 ounces to 1 pound

Records: NC—5 pounds, 7 ounces, Diversion Cannel, 1998; SC—4 pounds, 6 ounces, Lookout Shoals Lake, 1988; North America—5 pounds, 7 ounces, Diversion Canal, North Carolina, 1998

Notes: The Redear is a large, highly-regarded Southern sunfish that has now been introduced in many northern states. The Redear is often found in dense vegetation where it feeds on snails attached to plant stems. This makes it somewhat harder to locate and catch than other sunfish. In addition, the Redear is more tolerant of brackish waters than other sunfish and is often found along the deep water edges of salt marshes and coastal stream mouths. Even so, the Redear is one of the most popular sunfish in the coastal plains of the Carolinas.

Description: brown to olive green back and sides, overall bronze appearance; round, pale spots on head and sides; red eye; cheeks scaleless or partly scaled; steeply angled forehead (lower in Rock Bass); thicker, heavier body than other sunfish; large mouth

Similar Species: Green Sunfish (pg. 148), Rock Bass (pg. 158), Warmouth (pg. 160)

Roanoke Bass

no scales on cheek

Rock Bass

scales on cheek

Roanoke Bass

no dark margin on anal fin

Rock Bass

dark margin on anal fin

Roanoke Bass

6 spines on anal fin

Green Sunfish

3 spines on anal fin

Warmouth

3 spines on anal fin

ROANOKE BASS

Ambloplites cavifrons

Centarachac

Other Names: rock sunfish

Habitat: warm, small rivers, creeks and streams with medium current and a rocky bottom

Range: southern Canada through the central and eastern United States to the northern edge of the Gulf States; in North Carolina, only present in the Tar, Roanoke, Neuse and Chowan drainages

Food: crayfish, aquatic insects and small fish

Reproduction: spawns when water temperatures reach the high 60s to 70s; males build a small, round nest in shallow water; males guard eggs and fry

Average Size: 8 to 10 inches, 16 ounces to 1 pound, 8 ounces

Records: NC—2 pounds, 11 ounces, Fishing Creek, Nash County, 1994, (not recorded as NA record); SC—none; North American—2 pounds, 7 ounces, Tar River, North Carolina, 1990

Notes: The Roanoke Bass is a large sunfish that inhabits only four river drainages, making it one of the most restricted sport fish in North America. Roanoke Bass are very similar in appearance to the much more widespread Rock Bass and were once even considered a subspecies. Unlike Rock Bass, which are frequently plentiful in lakes, Roanoke Bass prefer small, rocky streams. Though they are unknown to most panfish anglers, Roanoke Bass have a small, but ardent, following, particularly among fly fishermen.

157

Description: brown to olive green back and sides with overall bronze appearance; each scale on sides has a dark spot; red eye; thicker, heavier body than other sunfish; large mouth

Similar Species: Green Sunfish (pg. 148), Roanoke Bass (pg. 156), Warmouth (pg. 160)

Rock Bass	**Roanoke Bass**		**Rock Bass**	**Roanoke Bass**
no round, pale spots on sides	distinct round, pale spots		dark margin on anal fin	no dark margin on anal fin

Rock Bass	**Green Sunfish**	**Warmouth**
6 spines in anal fin	3 spines in anal fin	3 spines on anal fin

ROCK BASS

Ambloplites rupestris

Other Names: redeye, goggle eye, rock sunfish

Habitat: clear lakes and midsized streams with vegetation and firm or rocky bottoms

Range: southern Canada through the central and eastern United States to the northern edge of the Gulf States; common in western North Carolina

Food: crayfish, aquatic insects, small fish

Reproduction: spawns when water temperature reaches the high 60s to 70s; male builds a nest in coarse gravel in submerged vegetation less than 3 feet deep; male guards eggs and fry

Average Size: 8 to 10 inches, 8 ounces to 1 pound

Records: NC—1 pound, 14 ounces, Deep River, 1998; SC—none; North American—3 pounds, York River, Ontario, 1974

Notes: A common sunfish in clear lakes and streams of western North Carolina, the Rock Bass can be locally plentiful and is a good fighter. Nevertheless, few anglers target them, as its flesh is somewhat more strongly flavored than that of Bluegills. In both lakes and streams, Rock Bass are normally found over a rocky or gravel substrate, even when vegetation is present. Rock Bass are frequently found in schools that stay put, not moving from their home territories. Once these schools are located, Rock Bass are easy to catch.

Description: back and sides greenish-gray to brown; faint vertical bands; stout body; large mouth; red eyes; 3 to 5 streaks radiate from eyes; dark spots on dorsal and anal fins

Similar Species: Bluegill (pg. 144), Green Sunfish (pg. 148), Redear Sunfish (pg. 154), Rock Bass (pg. 158)

Warmouth

jaw extends to middle of eye

Bluegill

small mouth does not extend to eye

Green Sunfish

jaw does not extend to middle of eye

Warmouth

light margin on gill spot

Redear Sunfish

orange-red margin on gill spot

Rock Bass

dark gill spot lacks light margin

WARMOUTH

Lepomis gulosus

Other Names: goggle eye, widemouth sunfish, stumpknocker, weed bass

Habitat: heavy weeds in turbid lakes, swamps and slow-moving streams

Range: the southern U.S. from Texas to Florida and north to the southern Great Lakes region; common in the Piedmont and coastal plains of the Carolinas, uncommon in the mountain regions

Food: prefers crayfish, eats aquatic insects and small fish

Reproduction: when water temperatures reach the high 60s to 70s, males build nest in coarse gravel in submerged vegetation less than 3 feet deep; males guard eggs and fry

Average Size: 11 inches, 8 to 12 ounces

Records: NC—1 pound, 13 ounces, McLeods Pond, Richmond County, 1976; SC—2 pounds, 2.5 ounces, Clarendon County, 1973; North American—2 pounds, 7 ounces, Yellow River, Florida, 1985

Notes: This secretive sunfish is common in the shallow lakes and swamps of the Carolinas. Warmouths are solitary, aggressive sight-feeders that are often found around rocks and submerged stumps when not hiding in dense vegetation. They prefer cloudy water with a soft bottom and can withstand low oxygen levels, high silt loads and temperatures into the 90s. The Warmouth's small size keeps it off the radar of most fishermen, but it has a good flavor and is a scrappy, strong fighter on light tackle. **161**

Description: gray-black back; silver sides with 6 to 8 uninterrupted black stripes; front of dorsal fin separated from soft-rayed rear portion; lower jaw protrudes beyond snout

Similar Species: Striped Bass Hybrid (pg. 164), White Bass (pg. 162), White Perch (pg. 168)

White Bass	**Striped Bass**	**White Bass**	**White Perch**
single spine on gill cover	two spines on gill cover	horizontal black stripes	no stripes except on lateral line

White Bass	**Striped Bass**	**Striped Bass Hybrid**
single tooth patch on tongue	two tooth patches on tongue	two tooth patches on tongue

WHITE BASS

Morone chrysops

Other Names: lake, sand or silver bass, streaker

Habitat: large lakes, rivers and impoundments with relatively clear water

Range: the Great Lakes region to the eastern seaboard, through the Southeast to the Gulf and west to Texas; stocked in reservoirs in central and western Carolinas

Food: small fish

Reproduction: spawns in late spring or early summer; eggs spread in open water over gravel beds or rubble 6 to 10 feet deep; some populations migrate to narrow bays or up tributary streams to spawn

Average Size: 9 to 18 inches, 8 ounces to 2 pounds

Records: NC—5 pounds, 14 ounces, Kerr Reservoir, 1986; SC—5 pounds, 4.8 ounces, Lake Murray, 2006; North American—6 pounds, 13 ounces, Lake Orange, Virginia, 1989

Notes: The White Bass is native to the Great Lakes and was introduced into several large reservoirs in the Carolinas. It quickly became established and has since become one of the most popular sport fish in the region. Often, anglers gather in large numbers along streams during the spawning run. In addition, White Bass inhabit large lakes and rivers where they travel in schools near the surface. These schools can often be spotted by watching for seagulls feeding on baitfish driven to the surface by schools of bass. The flesh is somewhat soft but has a good flavor that can be improved if the fish are put on ice and chilled as soon as it is caught. **163**

Description: dark gray back; bright silver sides with 7 or 8 indistinct stripes; dorsal fin separated, front part has hard spines, rear part has soft rays; two tooth patches, one on back of the tongue

Similar Species: Striped Bass (pg. 166), White Bass (pg. 162), White Perch (pg. 168)

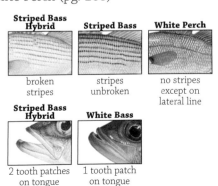

Striped Bass Hybrid — broken stripes

Striped Bass — stripes unbroken

White Perch — no stripes except on lateral line

Striped Bass Hybrid — 2 tooth patches on tongue

White Bass — 1 tooth patch on tongue

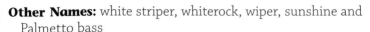

STRIPED BASS HYBRID

Moronidae

Morone saxatilis x Morone chrysops

Other Names: white striper, whiterock, wiper, sunshine and Palmetto bass

Habitat: open water of large lakes and slow-moving rivers

Range: stocked in about 40 U.S. states; the coastal plains and Piedmont of the Carolinas

Food: small fish, insects, crustaceans

Reproduction: hatchery-produced hybrid that is only occasionally fertile

Average Size: 1 to 2 feet, 5 to 10 pounds

Records: NC—17 pounds, 7 ounces, Lake Chatuage, 1996; SC—20 pounds, 6 ounces, Savannah River, 1978; North American—27 pounds, 5 ounces, Greer's Ferry Lake, Arkansas, 1997

Notes: There are two Striped Bass Hybrids. The Sunshine Bass is a hatchery cross between a male Striped Bass and a female White Bass. The Palmetto bass is the opposite; it is a cross between a male White Bass and a female Striped Bass. Both hybrids are fertile but there is only limited reproduction. Many states now raise large numbers of these hybrids to stock in waters too warm to support Striped Bass. This hard-fighting, tasty hybrid bass has now become a favorite with anglers in the Carolinas and across the country. The Hybrid Striped Bass is also becoming an important aquaculture fish, supplying filets for grocery stores as well as the restaurant market.

165

Description: dark gray back; bright silver sides with 7 or 8 distinct stripes; jaw protrudes beyond snout; dorsal fin separated, front part hard spines, rear part soft rays

Similar Species: Striped Bass Hybrid (pg. 164), White Bass (pg. 162), White Perch (pg. 168)

Striped Bass	**Striped Bass Hybrid**	**White Perch**
unbroken horizontal stripes	broken horizontal stripes	no stripes except on lateral line

Striped Bass	**White Bass**
two tooth patches on tongue	single tooth patch on tongue

STRIPED BASS

Moronidae

Morone saxatilis

Other Names: striper, streaker, surf bass, rockfish

Habitat: coastal oceans and associated spawning streams; landlocked in some large lakes and reservoirs

Range: the Atlantic coast from Maine to northern Florida, and the Gulf Coast; the coastal marine, coastal plains and Piedmont areas of the Carolinas

Food: small fish

Reproduction: spawns in freshwater streams; eggs deposited in riffles at the mouth of large tributaries; eggs must remain suspended to hatch

Average Size: 18 to 30 inches, 10 to 20 pounds

Records: NC—54 pounds, 2 ounces, Hiwassee Reservoir, 1991; SC—59 pounds, 8 ounces, Lake Hartwell, 2002; North American—78 pounds, 8 ounces, Atlantic City, New Jersey, 1992

Notes: Striped Bass are a coastal marine fish native to the Carolinas. Striped Bass are anadromous, which means they live in salt water and migrate into freshwater to spawn. When the Santee-Cooper Dam was built, it trapped some Striped Bass; these adapted to a freshwater existence and now spawn in tributary streams. Nevertheless, most of the introduced populations are maintained with hatchery-produced fish, with little or no natural reproduction. The introduction of the Striped Bass has created an exciting sport fishery. While the marine population of Striped Bass is declining, the "manmade" populations are thriving. **167**

Description: olive to blackish-green back; silver-green sides with no stripes; front spiny dorsal fin connected by a small membrane to the soft ray back portion

Similar Species: Striped Bass (pg. 166), Striped Bass Hybrid (pg. 164), White Bass (pg. 162)

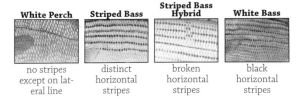

White Perch	Striped Bass	Striped Bass Hybrid	White Bass
no stripes except on lateral line	distinct horizontal stripes	broken horizontal stripes	black horizontal stripes

WHITE PERCH

Moronidae

Morone americana

Other Names: narrow-mouth bass, silver or sea perch

Habitat: brackish water in coastal areas; near-shore areas of the Great Lakes; expanding range into smaller freshwater lakes

Range: the Mississippi River drainage south to the Gulf of Mexico, Atlantic coast from Maine to South Carolina; coastal marine and plains of North Carolina and northern South Carolina

Food: fish eggs, minnows, insects, crustaceans

Reproduction: spawns in late spring over gravel bars of tributary streams

Average Size: 6 to 8 inches, 1 pound or less

Records: NC—2 pounds, 15 ounces, Falls of the Neuse Reservoir, 2001; SC—1 pound, 13.5 ounces, Lake Murray, 1996; North American—4 pounds, 12 ounces, Messalonskee Lake, Maine, 1949

Notes: The White Perch is a coastal Atlantic species native to the brackish waters of the Carolinas; however, it is quickly expanding its range into many freshwater habitats, often appearing in places where it is unwanted. It is very popular in some regions and hated in others. A small, schooling panfish, the White Perch migrates up coastal streams to spawn. The flesh is firm and white with a good flavor.

Description: olive green back; sides yellow-brown; many dark bars on side; slender fish with pelvic, dorsal and anal fins well back on body; snout flattened on top; rounded tail; upturned mouth; star-shaped blotch on top of head

Similar Species: Brook Silverside (pg. 110), Mosquitofish (pg. 62)

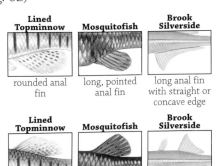

Lined Topminnow	**Mosquitofish**	**Brook Silverside**
rounded anal fin	long, pointed anal fin	long anal fin with straight or concave edge

Lined Topminnow	**Mosquitofish**	**Brook Silverside**
single dorsal fin	single dorsal fin	two dorsal fins

LINED TOPMINNOW
Fudulus lineolatus

Other Names: starred or lined killifish, starhead minnow

Habitat: surface of stream backwaters, swamps and pond edges with good vegetation

Range: Maritime provinces of Canada south through the Carolinas and west to Idaho; common in the Carolina coastal plains

Food: insects and crustaceans

Reproduction: from early spring through summer, males defend territories among weeds at stream or pond edges; eggs attach to the vegetation to hatch unattended

Average Size: 2 to 3 inches

Records: none

Notes: As the name implies, "topminnows" inhabit the upper water column and are adapted to feeding on or near the surface. Though inconspicuous and well camouflaged, they are the favorite target of wading birds. The Lined Topminnow is common and can be very abundant in the coastal plains, but is not found in brackish water, as many other topminnow species are. They withstand low oxygen levels well and are often used as bait minnows. Though not very colorful, they make good aquarium fish and readily eat food spread on the water's surface.

GLOSSARY

adipose fin a small, fleshy fin without rays, located on the midline of the fish's back between the dorsal fin and the tail

air bladder a balloon-like organ located in the gut area of a fish, used to control buoyancy—and in the respiration of some species such as gar; also called "swim bladder" or "gas bladder"

alevin a newly hatched fish that still has its yolk sac

anadromous a fish that hatches in freshwater, migrates to the ocean, then re-enters streams or rivers from the sea (or large inland body of water) to spawn

anal fin a single fin located on the underside near the tail

annulus marks or rings on the scales, spine, vertebrae or otoliths that scientists use to determine a fish's age

anterior toward the front of a fish, opposite of posterior

bands horizontal markings running lengthwise along the side of a fish

barbel thread-like sensory structures on a fish's head often near the mouth, commonly called "whiskers"; used for taste or smell

bars vertical markings on the side of a fish

benthic organisms living in or on the bottom of a body of water

brood swarm a large group or "cloud" of young fish such as Black Bullheads

carnivore a predatory fish that feeds on other fish (also called a piscivore) or animals

catadromous a fish that lives in freshwater and migrates into saltwater to spawn, such as the American Eel

caudal fin the tail or tail fin

caudal peduncle the portion of the fish's body located between the anal fin and the beginning of the tail

coldwater referring to a species or environment; in fish, often a species of trout or salmon found in water that rarely exceeds 70 degrees F; also used to describe a lake or river according to average summer temperature

copepod a small (less than 2 mm) crustacean, part of the zooplankton community

crustacean a crayfish, water flea, crab or other animal belonging to group of mostly aquatic species that have paired antennae, jointed legs and an exterior skeleton (exoskeleton); common food for many fish

dorsal relating to the top of the fish, on or near the back; opposite of the ventral, or lower, part of the fish

dorsal fin the fin or fins located along the top of a fish's back

eddy a circular water current, often created by an obstruction

epilimnion the warm, oxygen-rich upper layer of water in a thermally stratified lake

exotic a foreign species, not native to a watershed, such as the Zebra Mussel

fingerling a juvenile fish, generally 1 to 10 inches in length, in its first year of life

fork length the overall length of fish from mouth to the deepest part of the tail notch

fry recently hatched young fish that have already absorbed their yolk sacs

game fish a species regulated by laws for recreational fishing

gills organs used in aquatic respiration (breathing)

gill cover large bone covering the fish's gills, also called opercle or operculum

gill flap also called ear flap; fleshy projection on the back edge of the gill cover of some fish such as Bluegill

gill raker a comblike projection from the gill arch

harvest fish that are caught and kept by recreational or commercial anglers

hypolimnion bottom layer of the water column in a thermally stratified lake (common in summer); usually depleted of oxygen by decaying matter and inhospitable to most fish

ichthyologist a scientist who studies fish

invertebrates animals without backbones, such as insects, leeches and earthworms

kype hooked jaw acquired by some trout and salmon mainly during breeding season

lateral line a series of pored scales along the side of a fish that contain organs used to detect vibrations

littoral zone the part of a lake that is less than 15 feet in depth; this important and often vulnerable area holds the majority of aquatic plants, is a primary area used by young fish, and offers essential spawning habitat for most warmwater fishes such as Walleye and Largemouth Bass

mandible lower jaw

maxillary upper jaw

milt semen of a male fish that fertilizes the female's eggs during the spawning process

mollusk an invertebrate with a smooth, soft body such as a clam or a snail, often having an outer shell

native an indigenous or naturally occurring species

omnivore a fish or animal that eats plants and animal matter

opercle the bone covering the gills, also called the gill cover or operculum

otolith calcium concentration found in the inner ear of fish; used to determine age of some fish; also called ear bone

small freshwater game fish that can be fried whole in a pan, such as Black
pie, Bluegill and Yellow Perch

toral fins paired fins on the side of the fish located just behind the gills

elagic fish species that live in open water, in the food-rich upper layer of the column; not associated with the bottom

pelvic fins paired fins located below or behind the pectoral fins on the bottom (ventral portion) of the fish

pheromone a chemical scent secreted as a means of communication between members of the same species

piscivore a predatory fish that mainly eats other fish

planktivore a fish that feeds on plankton

plankton floating or weakly swimming aquatic plants and animals, including larval fish, that drift with the current; often eaten by fish; individual organisms are called plankters

plankton bloom a marked increase in the amount of plankton due to favorable conditions such as nutrients and light

range the geographic region in which a species is found

ray, hard stiff fin support; resembles a spine but is jointed

ray, soft flexible fin support, sometimes branched

redd a nest-like depression made by a male or female fish during the spawn, often refers to nest of trout and salmon species

riprap rock or concrete used to protect a lakeshore or river's bank from erosion

roe fish eggs

scales small, flat plates covering the outer skin of many fish

Secchi disc an 8- to 12-inch-diameter, black-and-white circular disc used to measure water clarity; scientists record the average depth at which the disc disappears from sight when lowered into the water

silt small, easily disturbed bottom particles smaller than sand but larger than clay

siltation the accumulation of soil particles

spawning the process of fish reproduction; involves females laying eggs and males fertilizing them to produce young fish

spine stiff, non-jointed structures found along with soft rays in some fins

spiracle an opening on the posterior portion of the head above and behind the eye

standard length length of the fish from the mouth to the end of the vertebral column

stocking the purposeful, artificial introduction of a fish species into a body of water

substrate bottom composition of a lake, stream or river

subterminal mouth a mouth below the snout of the fish

swim bladder see air bladder

tailrace area of water immediately downstream of a dam or power plant

terminal mouth forward facing

thermocline middle layer of water in a stratified lake, typically oxygen rich, characterized by a sharp drop in temperature; often the lowest depth at which fish can be routinely found

total length length of fish from the mouth to the tail compressed to its fullest length

tributary a stream that feeds into another stream, river or lake

turbid cloudy; water clouded by suspended sediments or plant matter that limits visibility and the passage of light

velocity the speed of water flowing in a stream or river

vent the opening at the end of the digestive tract

ventral the underside of the fish

vertebrate an animal with a backbone

warmwater a non-salmonid species of fish that lives in water that routinely exceeds 70 degrees F; also used to describe a lake or river according to average summer temperature

yolk the part of an egg containing food for the developing fish

zooplankton the animal component of plankton; tiny animals that float or swim weakly; common food for small fish

179

180

PRIMARY REFERENCES

Jenkins, R. E. and Burkhead, N. M
Freshwater Fishes of Virginia
American Fisheries Society, 2007

Lee, D. S. et al.
Atlas of North American Freshwater Fishes
North Carolina State Museum of Natural History, 1980

McClane, A. J.
Freshwater Fishes of North America
Henry Holt and Company, 1978

Menhinick, E. F.
The Freshwater Fishes of North Carolina
North Carolina Wildlife Resources Commission, 1991

Page, L. M. and Burr, B. M.
Freshwater Fishes, Peterson Field Guide
Houghton Mifflin Company, 1991

Rohde, F. C., R.G. Arndt, D.G. Lindquist & J.F. Parnell
Freshwater Fishes of the Carolinas, Virginia, Maryland, & Delaware
The University of North Carolina Press, 1996

ABOUT THE AUTHOR

Dave Bosanko was born in Kansas and studied engineering before following his love of nature to degrees in biology and chemistry from Emporia State University. He spent thirty years as staff biologist at two of the University of Minnesota's field stations. Though his training was in mammal physiology, Dave worked on a wide range of research projects ranging from fish, bird and mammal population studies to experiments with biodiversity and prairie restoration. A lifelong fisherman and avid naturist, he is now spending his retirement writing, fishing and traveling.